Beginning Linux SysAdmin

Getting Started with Linux System Administration

Neville Asiago Ondara

Apress®

Beginning Linux SysAdmin: Getting Started with Linux System Administration

Neville Asiago Ondara
Thika, Kenya

ISBN-13 (pbk): 979-8-8688-2162-2
https://doi.org/10.1007/979-8-8688-2163-9

ISBN-13 (electronic): 979-8-8688-2163-9

Copyright © 2025 by Neville Asiago Ondara

This work is subject to copyright. All rights are reserved by the Publisher, whether the whole or part of the material is concerned, specifically the rights of translation, reprinting, reuse of illustrations, recitation, broadcasting, reproduction on microfilms or in any other physical way, and transmission or information storage and retrieval, electronic adaptation, computer software, or by similar or dissimilar methodology now known or hereafter developed.

Trademarked names, logos, and images may appear in this book. Rather than use a trademark symbol with every occurrence of a trademarked name, logo, or image we use the names, logos, and images only in an editorial fashion and to the benefit of the trademark owner, with no intention of infringement of the trademark.

The use in this publication of trade names, trademarks, service marks, and similar terms, even if they are not identified as such, is not to be taken as an expression of opinion as to whether or not they are subject to proprietary rights.

While the advice and information in this book are believed to be true and accurate at the date of publication, neither the authors nor the editors nor the publisher can accept any legal responsibility for any errors or omissions that may be made. The publisher makes no warranty, express or implied, with respect to the material contained herein.

> Managing Director, Apress Media LLC: Welmoed Spahr
> Acquisitions Editor: James Robinson-Prior
> Development Editor: James Markham
> Editorial Assistant: Gryffin Winkler

Cover designed by eStudioCalamar

Cover image designed by Pexels

Distributed to the book trade worldwide by Springer Science+Business Media New York, 1 New York Plaza, New York, NY 10004. Phone 1-800-SPRINGER, fax (201) 348-4505, e-mail orders-ny@springer-sbm.com, or visit www.springeronline.com. Apress Media, LLC is a Delaware LLC and the sole member (owner) is Springer Science + Business Media Finance Inc (SSBM Finance Inc). SSBM Finance Inc is a **Delaware** corporation.

For information on translations, please e-mail booktranslations@springernature.com; for reprint, paperback, or audio rights, please e-mail bookpermissions@springernature.com.

Apress titles may be purchased in bulk for academic, corporate, or promotional use. eBook versions and licenses are also available for most titles. For more information, reference our Print and eBook Bulk Sales web page at http://www.apress.com/bulk-sales.

Any source code or other supplementary material referenced by the author in this book is available to readers on GitHub. For more detailed information, please visit https://www.apress.com/gp/services/source-code.

If disposing of this product, please recycle the paper.

To my family, mentors, and the vibrant open source community—thank you for your endless support, guidance, and inspiration throughout this journey. Your encouragement gave me the strength to keep writing even when it felt impossible.

Table of Contents

About the Author xvii

About the Technical Reviewer xix

Acknowledgments xxi

Introduction xxiii

Chapter 1: Introduction to Linux Administration 1

   Choosing and Setting Up Linux Distributions 1

   What Is a Linux Distribution? 1

   Major Types of Linux Distributions 2

      Debian-Based Distributions 2

      Red Hat–Based Distributions 2

      Arch-Based Distributions 2

      SUSE-Based Distributions 3

      Choosing the Right Linux Distribution 3

      Desktop vs. Server Distributions 3

   Installing and Setting Up Linux 4

      Selecting How to Install Linux 4

      Downloading the Linux ISO File 4

      Creating a Bootable USB Drive 5

      Booting from USB 9

      Installing Linux 10

   Command-Line Essentials 19

      What Is the Terminal? 19

      Basic Structure of a Command 20

TABLE OF CONTENTS

Must-Know Linux Commands 20

Real-World Scenario: Managing a Server via SSH 26

Key Takeaways 27

Chapter 2: Managing User Accounts 29

What Is sudo? 29

Introduction to Linux Users 29

Creating New Users 30

Creating a New User with useradd 30

Creating a User with adduser 31

Changing a Username 31

Changing a User's Home Directory 32

Deleting Users 32

Managing Groups 33

Creating a Group 33

Adding Users to a Group 33

Checking Group Memberships 33

Understanding File Permissions 34

Changing Permissions with chmod 34

Changing Ownership with chown 35

Enforcing Strong Password Policies 35

Real-World Scenario: New Employee Onboarding 36

Key Takeaways 37

Chapter 3: Filesystem Management 39

Understanding the Linux Filesystem Hierarchy 39

Checking Disk Usage 40

Disk Partitioning 41

Partitioning a Disk with fdisk 42

Creating a Filesystem Partition on /dev/sdb 42

Formatting Partitions 42

Mounting and Unmounting Filesystems 43

TABLE OF CONTENTS

 Manually Mount a Drive 44

 Unmount the Drive 44

 Making Mounts Permanent with /etc/fstab 44

Creating and Managing Swap Space 44

 Check Current Swap Space 44

 Creating a Swap File 45

 Swap and Hibernation 45

Monitoring Disk Health 46

 Check Disk IO Usage 46

 SMART Disk Health Check 46

Key Takeaways 47

Chapter 4: Basic System Configuration 49

Why System Configuration Matters 49

Managing System Services with systemd 49

 Understanding systemd Units 50

 Common Unit Types 50

 Example Services 50

 Starting the SSH Service (If It Didn't Auto-start) 51

 Verifying SSH Connectivity 52

 List All Services 52

 Check Failed Services 54

Process Management 55

 Viewing Running Processes with ps aux 55

 Real-Time Monitoring with top 56

 Enhanced Interactive View with htop 57

Managing Processes 58

 Killing a Process 58

 Sending Signals 59

 Adjusting Process Priority 60

 What Is "nice"? 60

 Job Control in the Shell 61

TABLE OF CONTENTS

    Basic Networking Setup 61

        Checking Network Interfaces 62

        Setting a Static IP Address (Ubuntu Netplan) 63

        Validating and Applying Netplan Safely 63

        Confirming the IP Address 64

        Testing Network Connectivity to the Local Gateway 64

        Testing Connectivity to an External Domain 65

        Checking DNS Resolution 65

    System Time and Time Zone Configuration 66

        Setting the Time Zone 66

        Synchronizing Time with NTP or Chrony 67

        apt vs. apt-get in Scripts 68

        Hardware Clock vs. System Clock 68

    Locale and Language Settings 69

        Viewing the Current Locale 69

        Setting the Default Language 70

    Automating Configuration with Scripts 71

        Notes on Automation 72

    Conclusion 73

Chapter 5: Package Management 75

    Understanding Package Management 75

    Placeholder and Example Policy 76

    Universal Package Management Wrappers 77

    APT/dpkg (Debian, Ubuntu, Linux Mint) 77

        APT Command Examples (Ubuntu 25.04) 78

    DNF/YUM/RPM (Fedora, RHEL, CentOS, AlmaLinux, Rocky Linux) 80

        Update Repositories 81

        Install Packages 81

        Update the System 81

        Remove Packages 81

        Clean Metadata 82

TABLE OF CONTENTS

- Auto-remove Unused Dependencies 82
- Search for Packages 82
- Add and Manage Third-Party Repositories (MySQL Example) 83
- Disable and Enable Repos 83

Pacman (Arch-Based Systems: Arch, Manjaro) 84
- Sync and Update 84
- Install Packages 84
- Remove Packages 85
- Force Remove Without Dependency Checks 85
- Clean Package Cache 85
- Search for Packages 86

Nix and Guix: Declarative, Atomic Package Management 86
- Nix 86
- Guix (GNU Guix System) 88

Snap and Flatpak: Containerized Desktop Packaging 89
- Snap 89
- Flatpak 90

Slackware-Based Systems (pkgtool/slackpkg, .tgz/.txz) 91
- Important Considerations 92
- Example: Manually Installing a Dependency 93
- Extending Slackware with Community Tools 93

Void Linux (XBPS, .xbps) 94

Solus (eopkg, .eopkg) 94

CRUX (pkgmk, pkgadd, .tar.gz) 95

GUI and Web-Based Tools for Package Management 95
- Synaptic Package Manager (Debian, Ubuntu, Linux Mint) 95
- Pamac (Manjaro, Arch Linux) 98
- Cockpit's PackageKit Plugin (Fedora, RHEL, AlmaLinux, Rocky Linux) 99
- NixUI/Guix Web Interfaces (NixOS, GNU Guix System) 100

Security and Auditing 102

Clarifying Edge Cases in Package Management 103

TABLE OF CONTENTS

Conflicts Between Snap, Flatpak, and Native Packages (APT/DNF/RPM) 103

Flatpak Permissions and Sandboxing Limitations 104

Managing Dual Systems (e.g., Flatpak + RPM on Fedora) 106

Conclusion 107

Chapter 6: Introduction to Shell Scripting 109

What Is Shell Scripting? 111

Why Shell Scripting Matters in Linux System Administration 111

Understanding the Shell 112

    Bash and Other Shells 112

    The Shell as a Command Interpreter 112

Shell Scripting Basics 112

    Creating Your First Shell Script 112

    File Permissions and the Shebang (#!) 113

    Running Scripts 113

Variables 113

    Declaring Variables 113

    Environment Variables 114

    Quoting: Single vs. Double 114

User Input and Output 114

    Echo and Print 115

    Command Substitution 115

Conditional Statements 115

    if, else, and elif 115

    test and [ ] Conditions 116

    Case Statements 116

Loops 116

    for Loops 117

    while Loops 117

    until Loops 117

Functions in Shell Scripts 118

    Returning Values 118

Error Handling and Debugging 118

    Exit Status 118

    Debugging with set 119

    Logging Errors 119

Automating Tasks with Shell Scripts 119

    Automated Full System Backup with Logging and Compression 119

    Automated Security Patch Installation with Reporting 121

    Server Resource Monitoring and Alert System 123

    Automated Log Analyzer and Report Generator 124

    Automated User Account Creation and Configuration 126

Scheduling Scripts with cron 128

    How cron Works 129

    Common Examples of cron Jobs 129

    Advanced Scheduling Patterns 130

    Permissions and Environment in cron 131

    Logging and Output 131

    Viewing Crontab Entries 132

    Remove Your Crontab 132

    Edit the System-Wide Crontab 132

    Viewing cron Job Logs 132

    Testing Your cron Jobs 133

    cron Troubleshooting Tips 133

    Real-World Use Case: Scheduled Backup with cron 133

Best Practices 135

Conclusion 135

Chapter 7: System Monitoring and Performance 137

Tools for Monitoring System Performance 137

    top, htop, and Other Monitoring Tools 137

Optional Enhancements 140

    Add pidstat for Per-Process Statistics 140

    iostat: Input/Output Statistics 140

TABLE OF CONTENTS

    free: Memory Usage Snapshot 142

    dstat: Versatile All-in-One Resource Monitor 143

When to Use Which Tool 145

Checking Memory and Disk Usage 145

    Memory Usage 145

    Disk Usage... 146

Analyzing System Resource Consumption 147

    Find High-CPU or High-Memory Processes 147

    Monitor Disk IO per Process with iotop 148

Managing System Logs 149

    Overview of Log Files (/var/log) 149

    Tips for Viewing Logs 151

    Using journalctl (for systemd-Based Systems) 151

    Rotating and Cleaning Logs 152

Identifying and Resolving Performance Bottlenecks 153

    Identifying High-Resource Processes 154

Performance Optimization Tips 155

    Disable Unused Services 155

    Clean Temporary Files 155

    Adjust Swappiness 157

    Use Lighter Desktop Environments 157

Tuning System Parameters 158

    Increase File Descriptors 158

    TCP Network Performance Tweaks 159

    Long-Term Monitoring Tools 161

Clarifications and Troubleshooting 164

    iostat and sysstat: Immediate vs. Historical Usage 164

    netstat vs. ss: Which to Use? 164

    Memory Metrics: "Used" vs. "Available" 164

    iotop Prerequisites and Troubleshooting 164

Linux Observability and Monitoring: Command Cheat Sheet 165

Conclusion 166

Chapter 8: Introduction to Security 167

Basic Security Concepts 167

    Confidentiality 167

    Integrity 167

    Availability 167

Key Definitions 168

Security Principles 168

    Least Privilege 168

    Defense in Depth 169

    Zero Trust 169

Common Linux Security Tools 169

    Popular Tools 169

Configuring Firewalls 170

    Introduction to iptables and firewalld 170

    Firewall Setup: Before You Start (iptables/nftables/firewalld) 170

    Packet Filtering with iptables, nftables, and firewalld 170

User Authentication and Authorization 174

    Understanding Authentication Methods 174

    Before You Start: SSH Hardening 174

    Password-Based Authentication (Default Method) 175

    Setting Up SSH Key Authentication 177

    Set Up Two-Factor Authentication (2FA) 180

Fail2Ban: Automatically Block Brute-Force Attacks 183

    What Is Fail2Ban? 183

    Step-by-Step Setup 183

Monitor Logins with auditd (Audit Daemon) 185

    Why Use auditd? 185

    Step-by-Step Setup 186

TABLE OF CONTENTS

Optional: Restrict SSH Access by IP Address 188
    Restrict SSH Access Using UFW 188
    Deny All Other SSH 189
    Check Status 189
Understanding AppArmor and SELinux (MAC Systems) 189
    What Is MAC (Mandatory Access Control)? 189
    SELinux: Security-Enhanced Linux 190
    AppArmor: Application Armor 193
    Which One Should You Use? 195
    Real-World Scenario: Hardening a Web Server 195
chkrootkit/rkhunter: Rootkit Detection Tools 196
    How to Detect Rootkits on Linux 196
    chkrootkit 197
    rkhunter (Rootkit Hunter) 198
    Best Practices for Rootkit Detection 200
    What to Do If You Suspect a Rootkit? 200
Conclusion 201

Chapter 9: Networking and Remote Access 203

Hostname and DNS Configuration 203
    Setting the Hostname 204
    Changing the Hostname 204
    Editing /etc/hosts and /etc/resolv.conf 205
    Editing /etc/resolv.conf 206
    systemd-resolved vs. resolvconf 207
    Viewing DNS Configuration with resolvectl 208
    How DNS Lookups Work on Linux 210
    Key Takeaways 211
    Static vs. Dynamic IP Addressing 211
Editing Network Configuration Files 212
    Debian/Ubuntu 212
    Configuring DNS with Netplan (/etc/netplan/*.yaml) 213

TABLE OF CONTENTS

Red Hat/CentOS/Fedora Networking 214

Package Management Note 216

Troubleshooting Network Interfaces 216

Check Interface and IP Address 217

Test Network Connectivity 217

Restart Interface or NetworkManager 217

View Logs from NetworkManager 218

Setting Up SSH for Remote Access 218

Installing SSH 218

Check SSH Service Status 219

Configure SSH Settings 219

Managing SSH Access Through Firewalls 220

SSH Connection and Key Authentication 221

Remote Access Logging and Monitoring 222

Understanding Linux Log Files for SSH 222

Using who, w, and last 223

Viewing SSH Service Logs with journalctl 224

Detecting Failed Login Attempts 225

Proactive Monitoring Tools 226

Remote Desktop and GUI Access 227

When Do You Need Remote GUI Access? 227

Option 1: Using VNC (Virtual Network Computing) 228

Using xRDP (Windows-Compatible Remote Desktop) 230

Running GUI Apps over SSH (SSH Tunneling) 231

Security and Performance Tips 233

Virtual Private Networks (VPNs) and Remote Connections 233

Log In and Download Config Files 234

Setting Up OpenVPN (Client) 235

Setting Up WireGuard on Ubuntu 237

Troubleshooting Tips 240

TABLE OF CONTENTS

Secure Remote File Transfer Using SCP and SFTP 240
    SCP (Secure Copy) 241
    SFTP (SSH File Transfer Protocol) 241
    Tips for Secure File Transfer 242
Conclusion 242

Chapter 10: Backup and Disaster Recovery 243
Backup Strategies 243
    The Importance of Regular Backups 243
Backup Tools: rsync, tar, and Others 244
    rsync: Remote Sync 244
    tar 248
    dd: Disk Duplicate 250
Cloud Backup Options 252
    Amazon S3 252
    Google Cloud Storage 260
    Backblaze B2 268
How to Test and Validate Your Backups 275
    For tar Archives 275
    For rsync 275
    For rclone 276
    For S3 276
Conclusion 276
Wrapping Up the Book 276

Index 279

About the Author

Neville Asiago Ondara is a passionate Linux enthusiast and system administrator with more than five years of hands-on experience in the realm of open source technologies. With a strong foundation in system architecture, scripting, and server management, he has helped countless individuals and organizations embrace the power of Linux for stability, scalability, and security.

Driven by a love for teaching and simplifying complex concepts, Neville has dedicated much of his career to mentoring beginners and making the Linux ecosystem more accessible. This book marks his effort to bridge the gap between curiosity and confidence for those starting their journey into system administration.

When he's not exploring the latest in open source tools or contributing to community forums, Neville enjoys tinkering with home lab setups and writing on tech in a way that empowers readers to learn by doing.

About the Technical Reviewer

Nikhil Kapoor brings more than 16 years of experience with a strong focus on Artificial Intelligence and Machine Learning, where he has designed and implemented advanced models, intelligent platforms, and data-driven solutions at scale. His expertise extends to architecting end-to-end platforms and distributed applications within a leading cloud service provider, integrating AI/ML capabilities with cloud-native technologies to drive innovation. He has applied these skills across diverse sectors—including finance, investment management, audit, and telecom R&D—delivering intelligent, scalable, and production-ready systems. In addition to technical depth, he has a proven track record of leading teams through the full software development lifecycle, coupled with strong communication and analytical skills that enable him to bridge technical complexity with business impact.

Acknowledgments

Writing *Beginning Linux SysAdmin* has been a journey fueled by support, curiosity, and community.

I would first like to thank my family for their unwavering belief in me and for creating an environment that nurtured both learning and perseverance.

A heartfelt thank-you to my technical reviewer, Nikhil Kapoor, whose expertise and insights were instrumental in shaping the quality and accuracy of this work.

I am grateful to the teams at Apress and Springer for their editorial guidance and for believing in the value of bringing foundational Linux knowledge to a broader audience.

To the global Linux community, your openness, collaboration, and shared passion for learning are what make open source truly powerful.

And finally, to every reader embarking on the Linux system administration journey: may this book be your trusted first step into a realm full of opportunity.

Introduction

Linux has become the backbone of modern computing, powering servers, cloud platforms, embedded devices, and more. As organizations continue to rely heavily on Linux-based infrastructure, the demand for professionals who can confidently manage, secure, and troubleshoot Linux systems is at an all-time high.

Beginning Linux SysAdmin: Getting Started with Linux System Administration is a practical, hands-on guide for readers who are either completely new to Linux or looking to formalize and strengthen their foundational system administration skills.

What This Book Covers

This book walks you through the core areas of Linux system administration, starting from the very basics and gradually introducing more complex topics. It's not just regarding theory; it's regarding real-world tasks that every system administrator will encounter in their day-to-day work.

The journey begins with an overview of the Linux ecosystem, its structure, and how to get your environment up and running. From there, you'll learn to manage users, configure filesystems, maintain systems, and secure your infrastructure. You'll gain exposure to shell scripting, performance monitoring, and disaster recovery strategies—building a robust toolkit as you progress.

Who This Book Is For

- IT professionals transitioning into system administration roles
- Students and hobbyists curious regarding Linux internals
- Developers and DevOps practitioners looking to understand the environments their code runs on
- Anyone with a beginning-to-intermediate-level interest in Linux system administration

INTRODUCTION

No prior Linux experience is required, though familiarity with basic command-line usage will certainly help.

Book Structure

The book is divided into ten chapters, each building upon the previous:

1. Introduction to Linux Administration: Understand what Linux is, its architecture, distributions, and core principles.

2. Managing User Accounts: Learn how to create, modify, and secure user accounts and groups.

3. Filesystem Management: Explore partitioning, mounting, and common file management techniques.

4. Basic System Configuration: Configure host names, time zones, system services, and startup behavior.

5. Package Management: Install, update, and manage software using popular package managers.

6. Introduction to Shell Scripting: Start automating tasks with Bash (Bourne Again SHell) scripting and command-line logic.

7. System Monitoring and Performance: Monitor CPU, memory, disk usage, and system health.

8. Introduction to Security: Learn basic Linux security best practices, firewalls, and user privilege management.

9. Networking and Remote Access: Configure networking interfaces, SSH (Secure Shell) access, and remote tools.

10. Backup and Disaster Recovery: Prepare for failure with data backup strategies and recovery techniques.

How to Use This Book

If you're completely new to Linux, I recommend reading the chapters in order. Each topic builds logically on the last and includes practical examples, commands, and summaries to reinforce learning. Intermediate users may prefer to head directly to chapters relevant to their current needs.

Wherever applicable, chapters include exercises and real-world scenarios to help reinforce your skills in a practical context.

A Note from the Author

Linux can seem intimidating at first, but once you break through the basics, you'll discover that it's one of the most powerful and rewarding operating systems (OSs) out there. My goal with this book is to help you cross that threshold with clarity and confidence.

Whether you're managing a personal server, exploring career opportunities, or simply curious regarding how Linux works, I hope this book becomes a valuable stepping stone in your journey.

—Neville Asiago Ondara

CHAPTER 1

Introduction to Linux Administration

Choosing and Setting Up Linux Distributions

One of the first things you'll notice when stepping into the Linux world is that there's not just one version of Linux—there are hundreds! These different versions are called distributions (or distros for short). Each one is built around the same Linux kernel but comes with its own set of tools, designs, and purpose.

In this chapter we'll explore the world of Linux distributions and help choose the right one for your needs. Once you've completed that, you'll see how to set up a Linux system and bootable USB stick and then learn the basic commands you'll use daily.

What Is a Linux Distribution?

Think of the Linux kernel as the engine of a car. The distribution is the full car, built around the engine, complete with the wheels, steering, and all the extra features you need to drive.

A Linux distribution bundles

- The Linux kernel (the core operating system)
- Software packages (utilities, libraries, desktop environments, etc.)
- A package manager (to install and update software)
- Configuration tools and documentation

Different distros are designed for different types of users and tasks—some are beginner-friendly, and others are built for advanced system administrators or security experts.

Major Types of Linux Distributions

Let's look at some of the most popular families of Linux distributions.

Debian-Based Distributions

- Examples: Ubuntu, Linux Mint, Kali Linux
- Known for stability, massive software repositories, and ease of use
- Ideal for beginners and anyone who wants a system that "just works"

Real-world tip: Ubuntu is a great choice for setting up a personal Linux workstation or a basic server.

Red Hat–Based Distributions

- Examples: Red Hat Enterprise Linux (RHEL), CentOS, Fedora
- Focused on enterprise use, reliability, and long-term support
- Common in corporate data centers and cloud environments

Real-world tip: If you're aiming for a job in enterprise IT or cloud administration, learning Red Hat-based systems will give you a strong advantage.

Arch-Based Distributions

- Examples: Arch Linux, Manjaro
- Designed for users who want full control over every part of their system
- Cutting-edge software, but with a steeper learning curve

Real-world tip: Arch is perfect if you love to tinker and want a deep understanding of how Linux systems are built from scratch.

SUSE-Based Distributions

- Examples: openSUSE, SUSE Linux Enterprise Server (SLES)
- Popular in businesses, especially for server and cloud infrastructure
- Known for powerful administration tools like YaST

Choosing the Right Linux Distribution

Here's a simple guide to help you pick:

If You Want …	Recommended Distribution
Easy to use for beginners	Ubuntu, Linux Mint
A stable, server-grade system	CentOS, Debian
The latest bleeding-edge software	Fedora, Arch Linux
Enterprise-level support and certification	Red Hat Enterprise Linux (RHEL), SUSE Linux Enterprise

Tip If this is your first Linux experience, start with Ubuntu or Linux Mint. They are user-friendly, well-documented, and perfect for learning.

Desktop vs. Server Distributions

Not all Linux systems come with a pretty desktop you can click around on. There's a huge difference between desktop and server distributions.

Desktop Distributions

- Come with a Graphical user interface (GUI) like GNOME, KDE, or XFCE
- Pre-installed with everyday apps (web browsers, email clients, office tools)
- Examples: Ubuntu Desktop, Fedora Workstation

Server Distributions

- Focused on performance, security, and stability
- No GUI by default—everything is managed from the command line
- Examples: Ubuntu Server, CentOS Stream

Installing and Setting Up Linux

Now that we've picked the perfect Linux distribution, it's time to roll up our sleeves and get Linux installed! In this section, we'll go step-by-step through setting up a Linux system.

Selecting How to Install Linux

You have two main options:

- Install Linux directly on your computer if you want it to be your main system or set up a dual boot.
- Install Linux inside a virtual machine (VM) if you want to practice safely without touching your main OS.

Tip I recommend using a virtual machine first if you're new. It's safe, quick, and lets you experiment freely.

Downloading the Linux ISO File

An ISO file is a digital copy of a Linux installation DVD. You'll need to download the ISO for your chosen distribution. Here's where to get them:

- Ubuntu: `https://ubuntu.com/download`
- Fedora: `https://getfedora.org/`
- Debian: `https://www.debian.org/distrib/`
- CentOS Stream: `https://centos.org/centos-stream/`

> **Note** Always download from the official website to avoid corrupted or unsafe files.

Creating a Bootable USB Drive

To install Linux on real hardware, you'll need a bootable USB stick. There are multiple ways to do this depending on your operating system. Let's walk through the most common methods.

For Windows: Use Etcher

You can use tools like **Balena Etcher** (https://etcher.balena.io/) to create a bootable USB from an ISO file. It is free and beginner-friendly. The following steps shows how to use Etcher:

1. Download and install **Etcher** from the official site.
2. Launch the application and click **"Flash from file."**
3. Select your ISO file (e.g., ubuntu-20.04.6-live-server-amd64.iso).
4. Insert your USB drive and click **"Select target."**
5. Choose your USB from the list.
6. Click **"Flash"** to begin writing the ISO.

> **Tip** Etcher works on Windows, macOS, and Linux—no installation needed if you use the AppImage.

Wait for the process to complete (Figure 1-1) and remove the USB safely.

CHAPTER 1   INTRODUCTION TO LINUX ADMINISTRATION

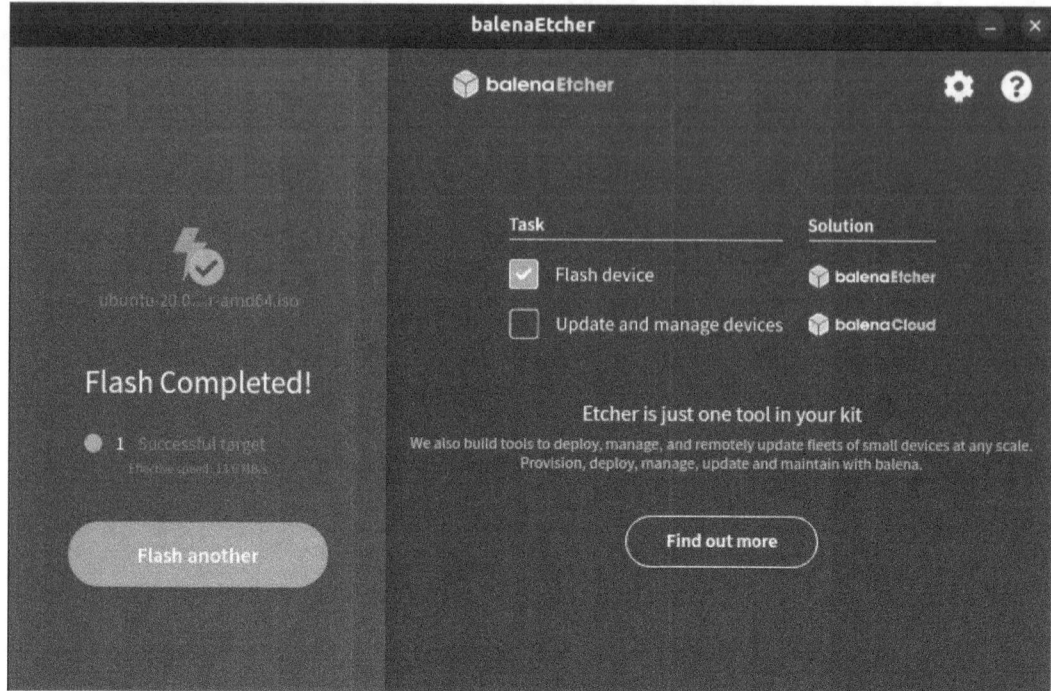

Figure 1-1. Balena Etcher application interface showing a complete flash process

For Windows: Use Rufus

If you're on Windows and prefer a lightweight tool, **Rufus** (rufus.ie) is another excellent option. It's especially good for flashing ISO images for legacy BIOS or UEFI boot systems.

Here is how to use it:

- Download Rufus from the official website.

- Insert your USB drive.

- Launch Rufus (no install needed).

- Under "Device," select your USB stick.

- Under "Boot selection," click "SELECT" and choose your ISO (e.g., `ubuntu-20.04.6-live-server-amd64.iso`).

- For most modern systems, leave **Partition scheme** as GPT and **Target system** as `UEFI (non-CSM)`.

- Click "Start" and wait for the flashing process to complete.
- When done, eject the USB safely.

Linux: Using `lsblk` and `dd`

The dd command is a powerful utility that serves multiple purposes, including copying, file conversion, and disk cloning. Additionally, it can be used to back up and restore data between devices.

Plug in your USB stick and list your block devices:

```
lsblk
NAME       MAJ:MIN RM  SIZE RO TYPE MOUNTPOINT
sda         8:0     0  500G  0 disk
├─sda1      8:1     0  450G  0 part /
├─sda2      8:2     0   50G  0 part /home
sdb         8:16    1   16G  0 disk
└─sdb1      8:17    1   16G  0 part /media/user/USB
```

Here, sdb is the USB device.

Unmount the USB partitions:

Before writing to the USB, unmount any mounted partitions:

```
sudo umount /dev/sdb1
```

If the USB has multiple partitions, unmount each one (e.g., /dev/sdb1, /dev/sdb2, etc.).

Write the ISO to the USB:

Now use the dd command to write the ISO image to the entire USB device:

```
sudo dd if=ubuntu-20.04.6-live-server-amd64.iso of=/dev/sdb bs=4M status=progress conv=fsync
1166407680 bytes (1.2 GB, 1.1 GiB) copied, 9.876 s, 118 MB/s
278+1 records in
278+1 records out
1166407680 bytes (1.2 GB, 1.1 GiB) copied, 9.876 s, 118 MB/s
```

CHAPTER 1 INTRODUCTION TO LINUX ADMINISTRATION

```
Replace ubuntu-20.04.6-live-server-amd64.iso with the actual name of your
ISO file
Replace /dev/sdb with the correct path to your USB drive (not a partition
like /dev/sdb1)
```

The flags `bs=4M` and `conv=fsync` improve performance and ensure data is fully written before removal.

macOS: Using `diskutil` and `dd`

If you're on macOS, the process of writing a bootable USB is similar but uses different commands and device names.

List your disks:

```
diskutil list
/dev/disk0 (internal): #: TYPE NAME SIZE IDENTIFIER 0: GUID_partition_
scheme *500.3 GB disk0 1: EFI EFI 314.6 MB disk0s1 2: Apple_APFS Container
disk1 500.0 GB disk0s2
/dev/disk2 (external, physical): #: TYPE NAME SIZE IDENTIFIER 0: FDisk_
partition_scheme *16.0 GB disk2 1: DOS_FAT_32 UNTITLED 16.0 GB disk2s1
```

Here, disk2 is the USB drive.

Unmount the USB:

To safely prepare the disk for writing, unmount the entire device:

```
diskutil unmountDisk /dev/disk2
```

Tip diskutil uses full disk identifiers like disk2, not partitions like disk2s1. Always unmount the entire disk before flashing.

Write the ISO to the USB:

On macOS, it's best to use the rdisk version of the device for faster write speeds:

```
sudo dd if=ubuntu-20.04.6-live-server-amd64.iso of=/dev/rdisk2 bs=4m
status=progress conv=sync
1124073472 bytes (1.1 GB, 1.0 GiB) copied, 9 s, 125 MB/s
```

```
300+1 records in
300+1 records out
1577058304 bytes transferred in 11.928737 secs (132204969 bytes/sec)
```

Replace ubuntu-20.04.6-live-server-amd64.iso and /dev/rdisk2 with your actual ISO file name and USB device path.

Warning   Be extremely careful when using dd. Choosing the wrong device can wipe your hard drive.

Booting from USB

Once your USB is ready:

1. Reboot your computer.
2. Enter **BIOS/UEFI** (typically via F2, F12, ESC, or DEL).
3. Set the **USB drive** as the first boot option.
4. Save and exit.

Your system should now boot into the Linux installation screen.

Note   If Secure Boot is enabled, you may need to disable it temporarily.

Windows/BitLocker Warning   On some laptops with BitLocker enabled (commonly on Windows systems), changing the boot order or booting from a USB drive can trigger a BitLocker recovery prompt. Make sure you have your BitLocker recovery key handy before proceeding, especially if you're dual-booting.

CHAPTER 1   INTRODUCTION TO LINUX ADMINISTRATION

Installing Linux

Once booted, follow the guided steps listed in Table 1-1.

Table 1-1. *Linux Installation Steps*

Step	Description
Language and keyboard	Select language and keyboard layout.
Network	Auto-configured via DHCP (Dynamic Host Configuration Protocol); optionally set static IP.
Archive mirror	Use default or change if needed for better speed.
Installation type	Choose base install (e.g., Ubuntu Server).
Disk partitioning	Use full disk (with/without Logical Volume Management (LVM)) or manual for advanced setups.
User setup	Create username, hostname, and strong password.
SSH access	Enable OpenSSH server if needed, or import SSH keys from GitHub/Launchpad.

Click **Install** and wait 10–20 minutes for completion.

Distribution Differences

The installation process outlined above is accurate for **Ubuntu Server**. Keep in mind that certain options may vary depending on the Linux distribution you are installing:

- Archive mirrors: The list of mirrors and the mirror selection interface differ by distribution.

- Disk and filesystem options: Support for Logical Volume Management (LVM) and advanced filesystems such as **ZFS** and **BTRFS** can vary. Some distributions may enable these features by default or require additional configuration.

- Installer interface:

  1. **Ubuntu Server** uses a **text-based installer** with menu-driven configuration steps.

  2. **Ubuntu Desktop** and **Fedora Workstation** provide a **graphical (GUI) installer**, which presents the installation process with windows, buttons, and visual feedback.

Installing with a GUI Installer (Ubuntu Desktop)

If you are using a desktop-focused distribution, the installation steps are similar but performed via a graphical user interface. Below is an example flow with screenshots for Ubuntu Desktop:

Keyboard layout:

Choose your keyboard layout as shown in Figure 1-2 and click **Continue**.

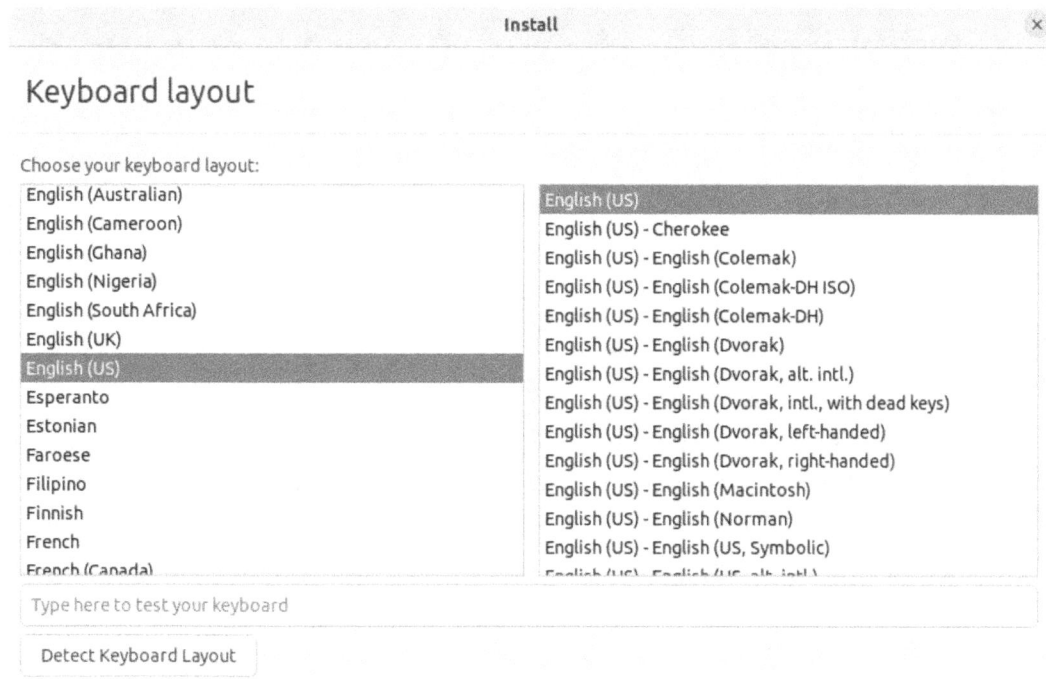

Figure 1-2. Choose a keyboard layout

CHAPTER 1   INTRODUCTION TO LINUX ADMINISTRATION

Updates and other software:

Select whether to install updates and third-party software as shown in Figure 1-3 and then click **Continue**.

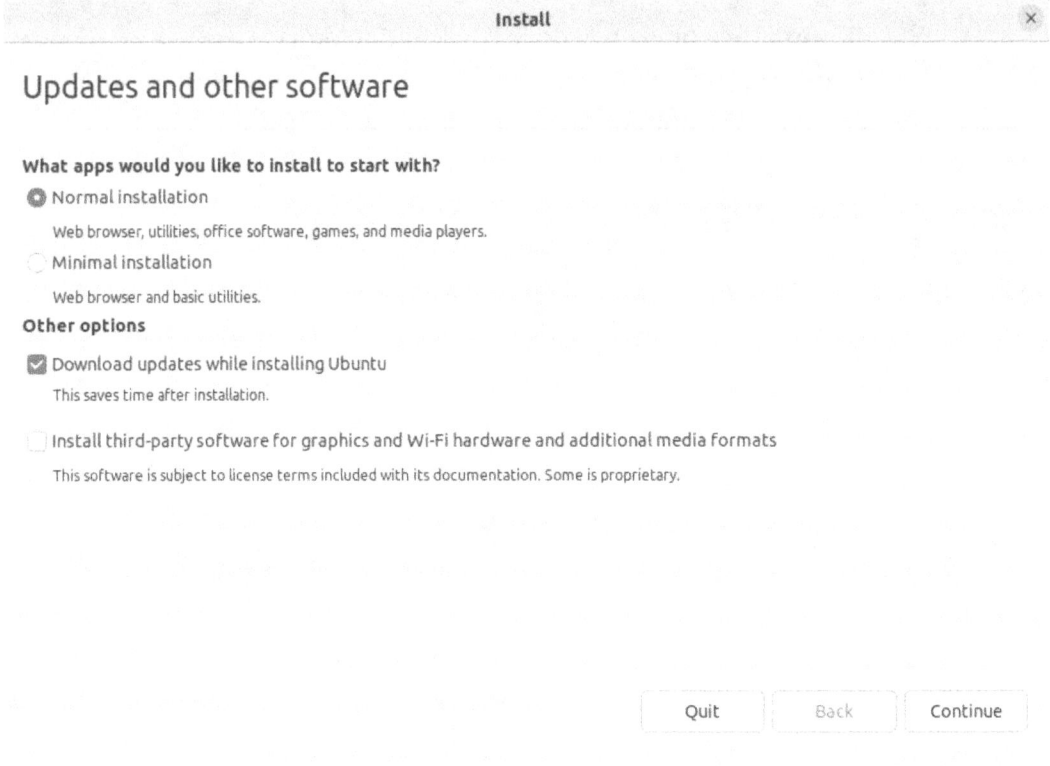

Figure 1-3. *Install updates and other software*

Installation type:

Choose the installation type (Erase disk and install Ubuntu or manual partitioning) and click **Install Now**. For this guide, we'll use the **Erase disk and install** option (see Figure 1-4).

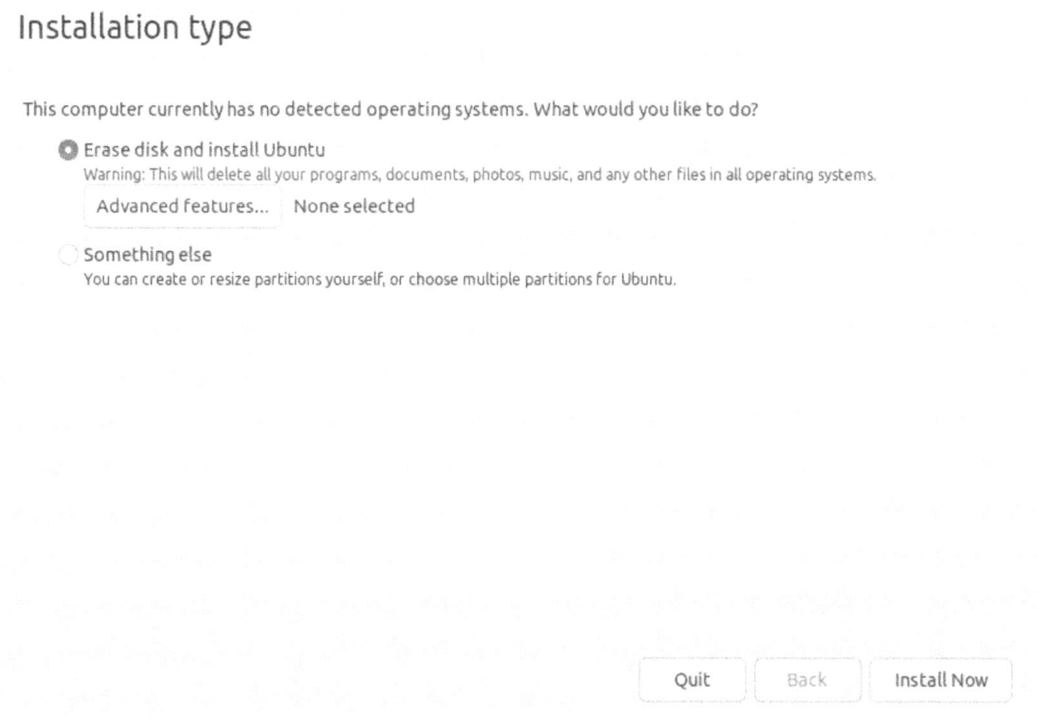

Installation type

This computer currently has no detected operating systems. What would you like to do?

◉ Erase disk and install Ubuntu
Warning: This will delete all your programs, documents, photos, music, and any other files in all operating systems.

[Advanced features...] None selected

○ Something else
You can create or resize partitions yourself, or choose multiple partitions for Ubuntu.

[Quit] [Back] [Install Now]

Figure 1-4. Erase disk and install Ubuntu

Note The **Erase disk and install Ubuntu** choice is the simplest and safest for beginners because it automatically handles partitioning and formatting for you. This means you don't have to worry about manually setting up partitions or filesystems, which can be complex and risky if done incorrectly. If you want more control over your disk layout or are setting up advanced features like LVM or encryption, you will use manual partitioning—but that's recommended only for experienced users.

Confirm changes:
In this prompt, click Continue to write changes to the disks (see Figure 1-5).

CHAPTER 1   INTRODUCTION TO LINUX ADMINISTRATION

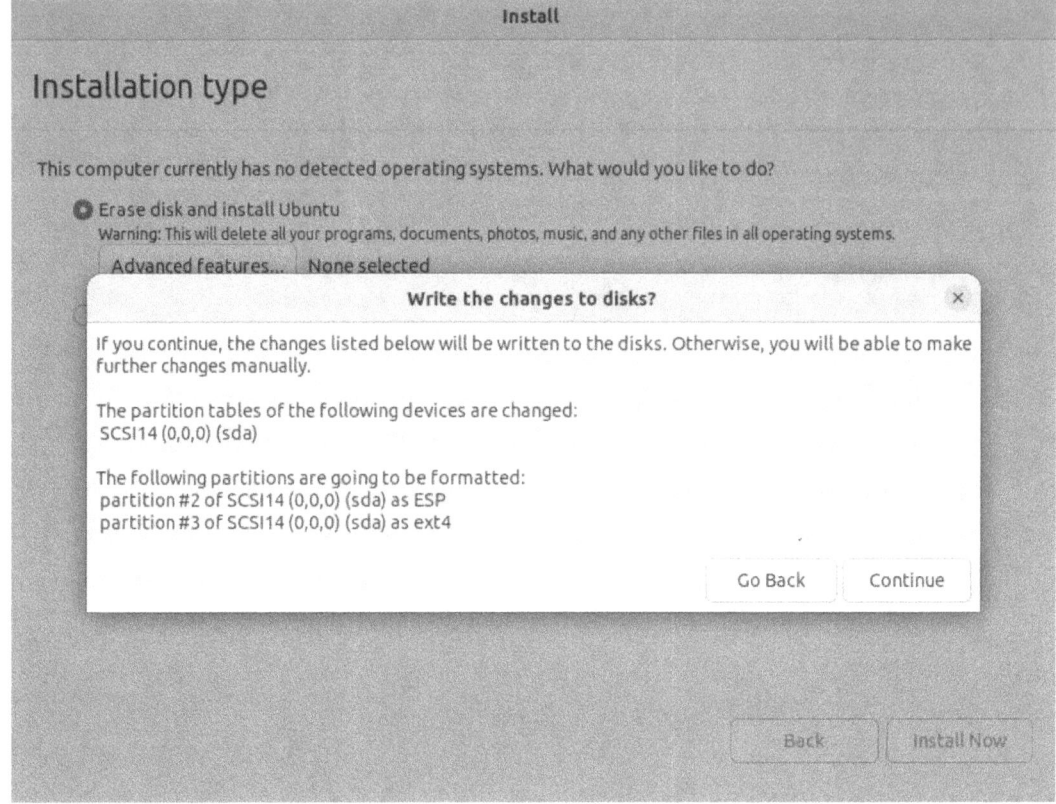

Figure 1-5. *Confirm changes*

Time zone:
Choose your location and time zone (see Figure 1-6).

CHAPTER 1 INTRODUCTION TO LINUX ADMINISTRATION

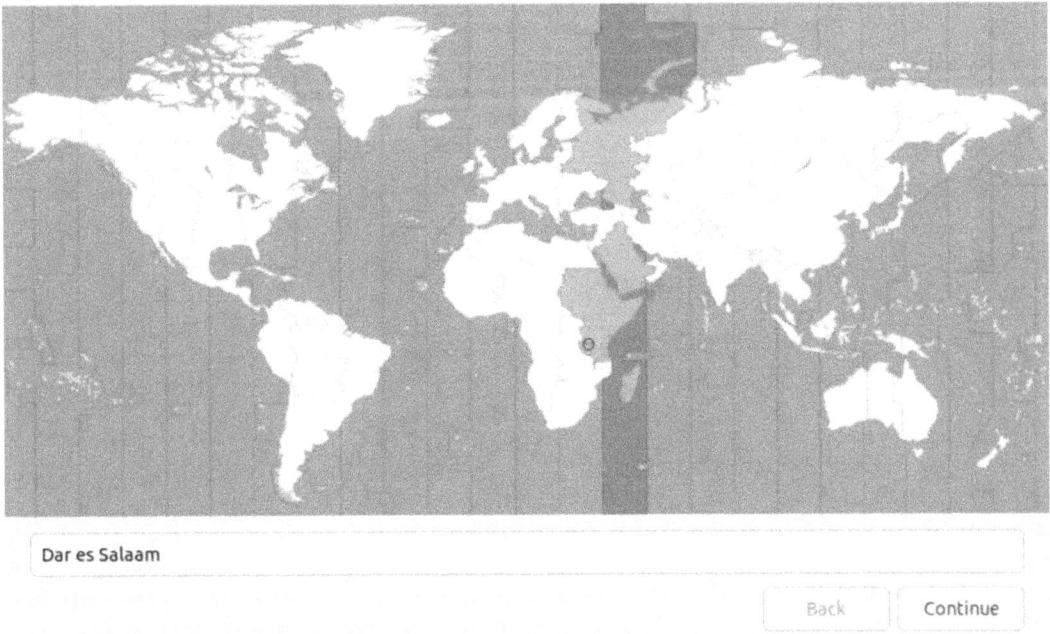

Figure 1-6. Select a time zone

User setup:

Create your username, computer name, and password and then click **Continue** (see Figure 1-7).

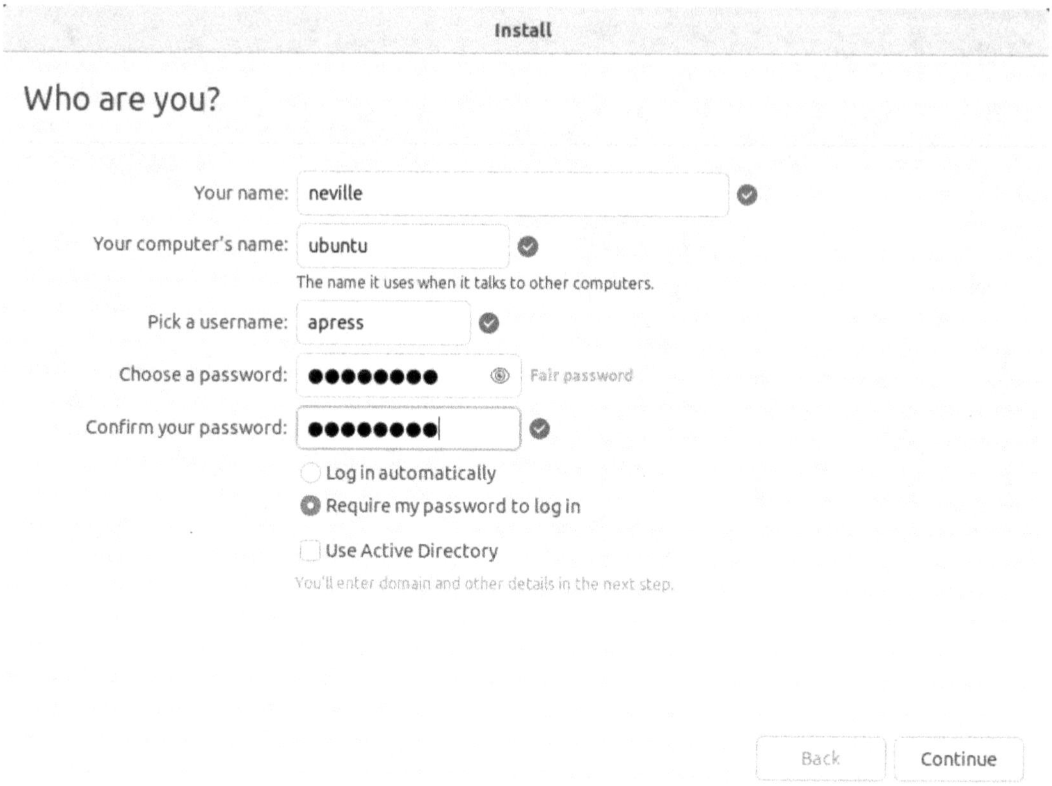

CHAPTER 1 INTRODUCTION TO LINUX ADMINISTRATION

Figure 1-7. Create a user account

Installation progress:

The installer will copy files and configure your system (see Figure 1-8).

CHAPTER 1   INTRODUCTION TO LINUX ADMINISTRATION

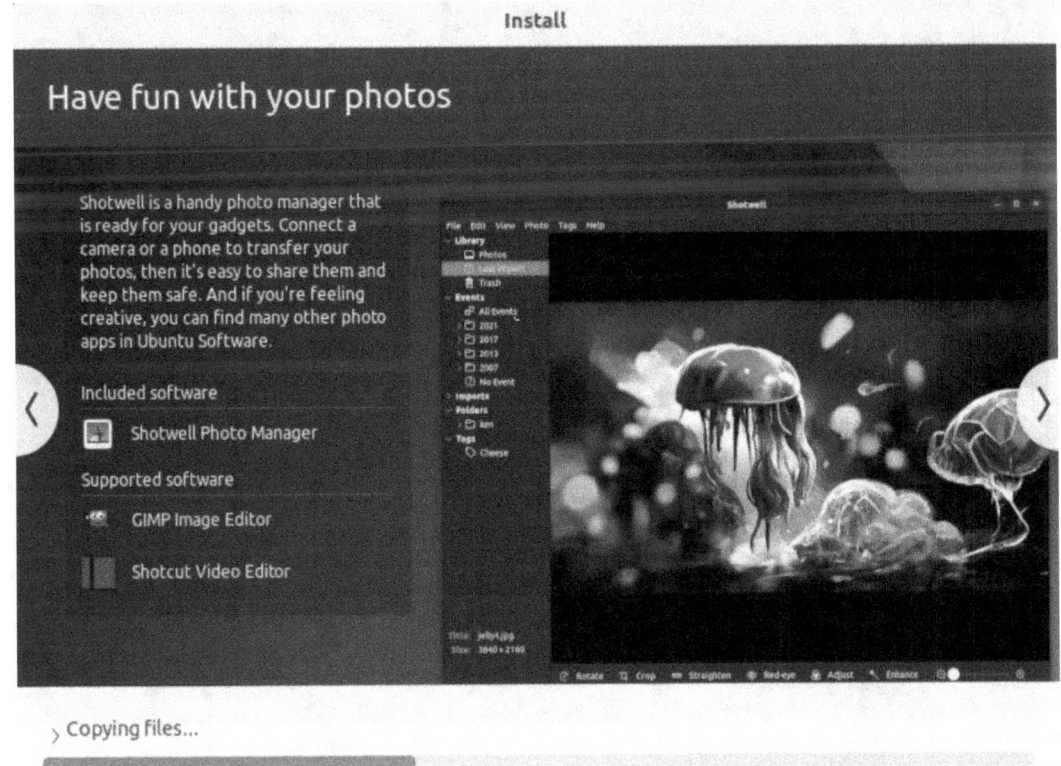

Figure 1-8. *Ubuntu installation progress*

Finish installation:
When complete, click the Restart Now button (see Figure 1-9).

CHAPTER 1   INTRODUCTION TO LINUX ADMINISTRATION

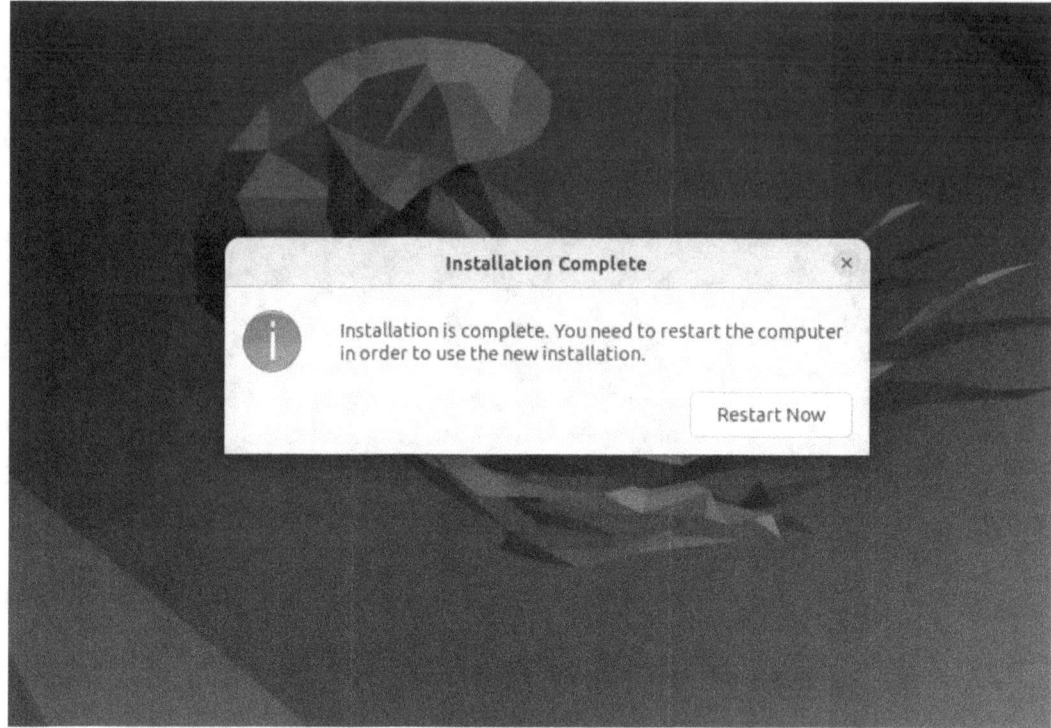

Figure 1-9. *Ubuntu installation completes*

Post-installation Setup

After installation is complete, follow these steps:

1. Remove the USB stick when prompted.
2. Reboot the system.
3. Log in with your username and password.

Once logged in, it's recommended to update your system packages to ensure you have the latest security patches and features. Run the following commands (or the equivalent for your distribution):

```
$ sudo apt update && sudo apt upgrade -y
```

To keep your system secure automatically, **enable unattended security updates** by installing and configuring the unattended-upgrades package:

```
sudo apt install unattended-upgrades
sudo dpkg-reconfigure --priority=low unattended-upgrades
```

This will prompt a configuration screen where you can enable automatic security updates. Once enabled, your system will automatically download and install critical security patches in the background.

Note If you're installing any Linux distro with a graphical interface, the process is quite similar—you'll still choose a language, configure the disk, set up a user, and install updates. The main difference is that the Desktop installer is GUI-based and more visual, whereas the Live Server installer uses a text-based menu.

Command-Line Essentials

If you want to become a skilled Linux administrator, the terminal is going to be your best friend. Sure, many Linux distributions offer beautiful graphical interfaces, but real power—the kind that lets you manage servers, automate tasks, and fix problems quickly—lies in the command line.

In this section, we'll learn the basic commands you'll use daily. Don't worry if you're new to this—we'll move step by step, and by the end, you'll be navigating Linux like a pro!

What Is the Terminal?

The terminal (also called the command-line interface, or CLI) is where you type instructions directly for the operating system to execute. It's incredibly powerful because it gives you full control over your Linux system.

Fun fact: Many professional Linux servers don't even have a graphical interface. Everything is done through the terminal!

You can open the terminal by

- Pressing Ctrl + Alt + T on most Linux desktops
- Searching for Terminal in the application menu

Basic Structure of a Command

A typical Linux command looks like this:

command [options] [arguments]

- command: The program you want to run.
- options (optional): Modify how the command runs. Usually prefixed with a dash -.
- arguments (optional): What the command should act on.

Example:

$ ls -l /home

- ls: List files.
- -l: Option for a long (detailed) listing.
- /home argument: The directory to list.

Must-Know Linux Commands

Let's get our hands dirty and try some! (See Tables 1-2 through 1-4 for command examples.)

Table 1-2. *Navigating the Filesystem*

Command	Purpose
Pwd	Print working directory (where you are).
Ls	List files and folders.
cd foldername	Change directory.
cd ..	Go up one level.
cd ~	Go to your home directory.

CHAPTER 1 INTRODUCTION TO LINUX ADMINISTRATION

Example:

```
$ pwd
/home/username
$ ls
Desktop  Documents  Downloads  Music  Pictures  Public  Templates  Videos
$ cd /etc
```

Table 1-3. *Managing Files and Directories*

Command	Purpose
touch filename	Create an empty file.
mkdir foldername	Create a new folder.
cp file1 file2	Copy a file.
mv file1 newlocation/	Move (or rename) a file.
rm filename	Delete a file.
rm -r foldername	Delete a folder and its contents.

Example: Create a new folder and move into it:

```
mkdir myfolder
cd myfolder
touch myfile.txt
ls
myfile.txt
```

Table 1-4. *Viewing and Editing Files*

Command	Purpose
cat filename	View the contents of a file.
nano filename	Open a simple text editor inside the terminal.
less filename	View a long file; scroll up and down easily.

CHAPTER 1　INTRODUCTION TO LINUX ADMINISTRATION

Example:

```
sudo nano myfile.txt
```

Type something, and then press Ctrl + O to save and Ctrl + X to exit.

```
cat myfile.txt
Hello, this is a test file!
```

Getting Help

Linux has built-in manuals for almost every command. If you ever forget what a command does, you can find help right away (Table 1-5).

Table 1-5. *Built-In Manual Commands*

Command	Purpose
man commandname	Read the manual page for a command.
command --help	Quick help summary for a command.

Example:

```
$ man ls
(Press q to quit the manual.)
$ ls --help
Usage: ls [OPTION]... [FILE]...
List information about the FILEs (the current directory by default).
Sort entries alphabetically if none of -cftuvSUX nor --sort is specified.
Mandatory arguments to long options are mandatory for short options too.
  -a, --all                  do not ignore entries starting with .
  -A, --almost-all           do not list implied . and ..
      --author               with -l, print the author of each file
  -b, --escape               print C-style escapes for nongraphic characters
      --block-size=SIZE      with -l, scale sizes by SIZE when
                             printing them;
e.g., '--block-size=M'; see SIZE format below
  -B, --ignore-backups       do not list implied entries ending with ~
```

| -c | with -lt: sort by, and show, ctime (time of last change of file status information); with -l: show ctime and sort by name; otherwise: sort by ctime, newest first |

......

Tables 1-6 through 1-10 list additional helpful commands from file permissions to disk usage and monitoring.

Table 1-6. File Permissions

Command	Purpose
chmod permissions filename.	Change file permissions.
chown user:group filename	Change file owner and group.

Example: Modify file permissions:

```
$ chmod 644 myfile.txt
$ ls -l myfile.txt
-rw-r--r--. 1 root root 717 May 02 17:50 myfile.txt
$ chown user:user myfile.txt
-rw-r--r--. 1 user user 717 May 02 17:50 myfile.txt
```

Table 1-7. Process Management

Command	Purpose
ps aux	View running processes.
top	Interactive process viewer.
kill PID	Stop a process by its PID.
htop	A more user-friendly top. Install with your package manager (e.g., apt, yum, pacman).

CHAPTER 1   INTRODUCTION TO LINUX ADMINISTRATION

Example: Check processes and terminate one:

```
$ ps aux
USER        PID %CPU %MEM    VSZ   RSS TTY      STAT START   TIME COMMAND
root          1  0.7  0.7  76796 28908 ?        Ss   17:25   0:53 /sbin/init splash
root          2  0.0  0.0      0     0 ?        S    17:25   0:00 [kthreadd]
root          3  0.0  0.0      0     0 ?        S    17:25   0:00 [pool_workqueue_release]
root          4  0.0  0.0      0     0 ?        I<   17:25   0:00 [kworker/R-rcu_gp]
root          5  0.0  0.0      0     0 ?        I<   17:25   0:00 [kworker/R-sync_wq]
root          6  0.0  0.0      0     0 ?        I<   17:25   0:00 [kworker/R-slub_flushwq]
root          7  0.0  0.0      0     0 ?        I<   17:25   0:00 [kworker/R-netns]
$ $ kill 1234  # replace with the actual PID
```

Table 1-8. *Networking*

Command	Purpose
ping hostname	Test network connectivity.
curl URL	Fetch a web page.
wget URL	Download a file.
ss -tulpen	Show active connections (may require sudo).

Note   The "ss" command is a modern replacement for "netstat." If "ss" or "netstat" is not available on your system, install "iproute2" or "net-tools" using your package manager.

Example: Test network connectivity:

```
$ ping google.com
PING google.com (216.58.223.110) 56(84) bytes of data.
64 bytes from mba01s08-in-f14.1e100.net (216.58.223.110): icmp_seq=1 ttl=117 time=16.2 ms
64 bytes from mba01s08-in-f14.1e100.net (216.58.223.110): icmp_seq=2 ttl=117 time=16.2 ms
64 bytes from mba01s08-in-f14.1e100.net (216.58.223.110): icmp_seq=3 ttl=117 time=199 ms
```

CHAPTER 1 INTRODUCTION TO LINUX ADMINISTRATION

```
64 bytes from mba01s08-in-f14.1e100.net (216.58.223.110): icmp_seq=4
ttl=117 time=378 ms
$ curl https://google.com
<HTML><HEAD><meta http-equiv="content-type" content="text/
html;charset=utf-8">
<TITLE>301 Moved</TITLE></HEAD><BODY>
<H1>301 Moved</H1>
```

The document has moved:

```
<A HREF="https://www.google.com/">here</A>.
</BODY></HTML>
```

Example: Archive and extract files:

Table 1-9. *Archiving and Compression*

Command	Purpose
tar -cvf archive.tar files	Create a tar archive.
tar -xvf archive.tar	Extract a tar archive.
zip archive.zip files	Create a zip file.
unzip archive.zip	Extract a zip file.

```
$ tar -cvf backup.tar myfolder
myfolder/
Myfolder/myfile.txt

$ tar -xvf backup.tar
myfolder/
myfolder/myfile.txt
```

Example: Use zip and unzip:

```
$ zip -r backup.zip myfolder
  adding: myfolder/ (stored 0%)
  adding: myfolder/myfile.txt (deflated 20%)

$ unzip backup.zip
  Archive:  backup.zip
```

```
creating: myfolder/
inflating: myfolder/myfile.txt
```

Example: Check disk space and folder size:

Table 1-10. Disk Usage and Monitoring

Command	Purpose
df -h	Show disk space usage.
du -sh foldername	Show folder size.
free -h	Display memory usage.

```
$ df -h
Filesystem        Size  Used Avail Use% Mounted on
tmpfs             383M  5.2M  377M   2% /run
/dev/sda2         458G   59G  376G  14% /
tmpfs             1.9G   25M  1.9G   2% /dev/shm
tmpfs             5.0M   12K  5.0M   1% /run/lock
tmpfs             383M  104K  382M   1% /run/user/1000
$ du -sh myfolder
4.0K    myfolder
$ free -h
              total        used        free      shared  buff/cache   available
Mem:           3.7Gi       2.8Gi       198Mi       289Mi       1.3Gi       963Mi
Swap:          255Mi       255Mi        40Ki
```

Real-World Scenario: Managing a Server via SSH

Imagine you are responsible for a company's remote web server. You connect via SSH (Secure Shell) and have no GUI—only the terminal.

You need to

- Navigate directories.
- Check configuration files.

- Restart services.
- Fix issues quickly.

That's why mastering basic commands is so important! It's the foundation of everything else you'll do in Linux administration.

Key Takeaways

- Linux comes in many flavors—each suited for different tasks.
- Ubuntu and CentOS are excellent starting points for beginners.
- Understanding whether you need a desktop or server setup will help you choose the right distribution.
- Use Etcher or Rufus for a user-friendly, GUI-based experience on Windows or macOS.
- On Linux/macOS, the dd command provides a powerful CLI method for creating bootable drives.
- Always verify the target device before writing an image to avoid data loss.
- Boot configuration (BIOS/UEFI) and Secure Boot settings can affect installation.
- This process is the entry point for deploying Linux on physical machines.
- The terminal gives you full control over Linux.
- Commands have a structure: command [options] [arguments].
- Practice navigation, file management, and reading help manuals.

The more you practice using the terminal, the more confident and powerful you'll become.

CHAPTER 2

Managing User Accounts

As Linux system administrators, one of our biggest responsibilities is managing users.

User management isn't just about creating accounts—it's about organizing users into groups, setting correct permissions, maintaining security, and ensuring the system runs smoothly.

Linux is built around a multi-user system, where different users have different levels of privileges. The root user (also called the superuser) has unrestricted access to the system, meaning they can install software, modify system configurations, and even delete critical files.

However, using the root account directly is risky—one wrong command could break the entire system. This is where sudo comes in.

What Is sudo?

sudo (short for Super User Do) is a command that allows a regular user to execute commands with root privileges temporarily. It ensures that only authorized users can perform administrative tasks while maintaining security.

In this chapter, we'll dive deep into creating, modifying, and securing user accounts, with lots of examples you can follow along with.

Introduction to Linux Users

In Linux, everything is based on users.

Every user has

- A username (e.g., neville)
- A User ID (UID)—a unique number identifying the user
- A Group ID (GID)—linked to their primary group

CHAPTER 2 MANAGING USER ACCOUNTS

- A home directory (e.g., /home/neville)
- A default shell (like Bash /bin/bash)

To list all users on the system:

```
$ cat /etc/passwd
root:x:0:0:root:/root:/bin/bash
daemon:x:1:1:daemon:/usr/sbin:/usr/sbin/nologin
bin:x:2:2:bin:/bin:/usr/sbin/nologin
sys:x:3:3:sys:/dev:/usr/sbin/nologin
sync:x:4:65534:sync:/bin:/bin/sync
```

Note Each line in /etc/passwd represents one user account.

Creating New Users

Adding new users is simple but powerful. Let's see how.

Creating a New User with useradd

To create a user:

```
$ sudo useradd -m -s /bin/bash alex
```

- -m: Create a home directory automatically.
- -s /bin/bash: Set Bash as the default shell.

Now set a password for the user:

```
$ sudo passwd alex
Enter new UNIX password:
Retype new UNIX password:
passwd: password updated successfully
```

Creating a User with adduser

To add a new user to the system, use the "adduser" command. This command also creates a home directory and prompts for user details:

```
$ sudo adduser james
info: Adding user `james' ...
info: Selecting UID/GID from range 1000 to 59999 ...
info: Adding new group `james' (1012) ...
info: Adding new user `james' (1012) with group `james (1012)' ...
info: Creating home directory `/home/james' ...
info: Copying files from `/etc/skel' ...
New password:
Retype new password:
passwd: password updated successfully
Changing the user information for james
Enter the new value, or press ENTER for the default
    Full Name []:
    Room Number []:
    Work Phone []:
    Home Phone []:
    Other []:
Is the information correct? [Y/n]
info: Adding new user `james' to supplemental / extra groups `users' ...
info: Adding user `james' to group `users' ...
```

You can leave most of it blank by pressing Enter.

Changing a Username

If a user's name needs to be changed, the "usermod" command lets you rename the account while keeping all files and settings:

```
$ sudo usermod -l newname oldname
```

　　Example: Rename james to alex_dev:

```
$ sudo usermod -l alex_dev james
```

Changing a User's Home Directory

After changing a username with usermod, the system does **not** automatically rename their home directory. To keep things consistent, you can manually rename the home folder to match the new username:

sudo mv /home/alex /home/alex_dev

Update the user's home directory path.

You can also update the user's home directory path using

sudo usermod -d /home/alex_dev alex_dev

This command tells the system that the user alex_dev's home directory is now located at /home/alex_dev.

Deleting Users

When a user account is no longer needed, it's important to remove it from the system carefully to avoid leaving orphaned files or clutter.

Linux provides a command to delete a user account along with their personal data, including their home directory and mail spool.

To delete a user and **remove their home directory and mail spool**, use the following command:

sudo userdel -r alex_dev

The -r flag ensures that the user's **home directory and mail files are also deleted**, freeing up disk space.

Warning Be very careful when deleting users with the -r option.

Once deleted, the user's files and data **cannot be easily recovered**.

Always double-check you have backed up any important data before proceeding.

Managing Groups

Groups make user management much easier. Instead of assigning permissions user by user, you can manage permissions at the group level.

Creating a Group

To create a new group, use the `groupadd` command. For example, to create a group called `developers`:

```
$ sudo groupadd developers
```

Adding Users to a Group

To add a user to a group without removing them from existing groups, use

```
$ sudo usermod -aG developers alex_dev
```

The `-aG` option appends the user to the group `developers`.

Checking Group Memberships

In Linux, every user belongs to one or more groups. Groups make it easier to assign permissions to multiple users at once, especially for shared projects or system administration tasks. To see which groups a user belongs to, we can use the `groups` command:

```
$ groups alex_dev
alex_dev : alex_dev users developers
```

In this example, the user **alex_dev** is part of three groups: the primary group `alex_dev` and the secondary groups `users` and `developers`.

Understanding File Permissions

Linux uses a system of permissions to control who can read, write, or execute files.

Try to run

```
$ ls -l notes.txt
-rw-r--r--. 1 root root 202 May 6 21:38 notes.txt
```

Breakdown:

- `-rw-r--r--.`: File permissions:
    - The first character (`-`) indicates this is a regular file.
    - The next three (`rw-`) are the **owner's permissions**: read and write.
    - The next three (`r--`) are the **group's permissions**: read only.
    - The final three (`r--`) are for **others**: read only.

Note The **trailing dot (.)** at the end of the permission string indicates that the file has an **SELinux context** (common on systems with SELinux enabled).

On other systems, you might see a **plus sign (+)** instead, which means the file has **Access Control Lists (ACLs)** applied.

Changing Permissions with chmod

To modify permissions, use the chmod command, for example:

```
$ chmod 755 filename.txt
```

```
This sets permissions to:
Owner: read, write, execute
Group: read, execute
Others: read, execute
Resulting permission line (if you run ls -l filename.txt):
-rwxr-xr-x. 1 root root 13 May  7 12:54 filename.txt
```

Changing Ownership with chown

To change the owner and group of a file:

```
$ sudo chown newowner:newgroup filename
```

Example:

```
$ sudo chown alex_dev:developers project.txt
```

Effect:

- Changes the file's ownership to
    - Owner: alex_dev
    - Group: developers

Resulting line from (ls -l project.txt):

```
-rw-r--r--. 1 alex_dev developers 567 May  6 22:15 project.txt
```

Enforcing Strong Password Policies

For security, it's important to enforce password rules like expiration, length, and complexity.

While you can edit /etc/login.defs to control some settings (like maximum password age and warning days), modern systems typically use **PAM modules** (such as pam_pwquality.so) to enforce password complexity and quality.

Example: Force a user to change their password every 90 days:

```
$ sudo chage -M 90 alex_dev
```

To check the result:

```
$ sudo chage -l alex_dev
Last password change                                    : May 06, 2025
Password expires                                        : Aug 04, 2025
Password inactive                                       : never
Account expires                                         : never
Minimum number of days between password change          : 0
Maximum number of days between password change          : 90
Number of days of warning before password expires       : 7
```

> **Tip** To configure password quality requirements, check your PAM configuration files (e.g., /etc/pam.d/common-password) and look for modules like pam_pwquality.so.

Real-World Scenario: New Employee Onboarding

Imagine your company hires five new engineers. You need to

- Create their accounts.
- Add them to the developers group.
- Enforce password security.

Instead of doing everything manually, you can script it!
Example script:
Open the terminal and use a text editor to create the file:

```
$ sudo nano onboard_developers.sh
```

Add the following lines to the script:

```
#!/bin/bash
for user in alice bob charlie dave eve
do
    sudo useradd -m -s /bin/bash $user
    sudo passwd $user
    sudo usermod -aG developers $user
done
```

Save and exit (in nano, press Ctrl + O, then Enter, and then Ctrl + X).
Make it executable:

```
$ chmod +x onboard_developers.sh
```

Run the script:

```
$ sudo ./onboard_developers.sh
New password:
Retype new password:
passwd: password updated successfully
New password:
Retype new password:
passwd: password updated successfully
New password:
Retype new password:
passwd: password updated successfully
New password:
Retype new password:
passwd: password updated successfully
New password:
Retype new password:
passwd: password updated successfully
```

You'll be prompted to set a password for each user in the list. Now you've saved hours of manual work!

Key Takeaways

- We create users with useradd or adduser.
- We modify users with usermod and delete them with userdel.
- We manage groups with groupadd, usermod -aG, and groupdel.
- Permissions and ownership are handled with chmod and chown.

User and group management is the foundation of Linux security, and now you're ready to do it confidently!

CHAPTER 3

Filesystem Management

In Linux, everything is a file—even directories, devices, and system information. Understanding the Linux filesystem is critical because it impacts system performance, data security, and server reliability.

In this chapter, we'll walk through the filesystem structure, disk partitioning, mounting drives, managing swap space, and monitoring disk health.

Ready? Let's get started!

Understanding the Linux Filesystem Hierarchy

Linux organizes everything under a single unified directory structure—called the Filesystem Hierarchy Standard (FHS).

Table 3-1 provides a quick overview of key directories.

Table 3-1. *Key Directories*

Directory	Purpose
/	Root directory—everything starts here
/home/	User directories (e.g., /home/neville)
/etc/	Configuration files for the system
/var/	Variable data (logs, mail, caches)
/usr/	User programs, libraries, and documentation
/bin/	Essential command binaries (e.g., ls, cp)
/sbin/	System binaries (e.g., mount, reboot)
/tmp/	Temporary files, cleared at reboot
/dev/	Device files (hard drives, USBs, etc.)

Example:
To view your filesystem:

```
$ sudo tree -L 2 /
/
├── bin -> usr/bin
├── boot
├── dev
├── etc
├── home
├── lib
├── media
├── mnt
├── opt
├── proc
├── root
├── run
├── sbin -> usr/sbin
├── srv
├── sys
├── tmp
├── usr
├── var
```

Running `tree /` may produce a lot of output and omit directories due to permissions. Use `sudo` for better results.

Checking Disk Usage

Before working with disks—such as partitioning or formatting—it's important to assess how your current storage is being used. This helps you identify space constraints, understand disk layout, and avoid data loss (see Table 3-2).

Table 3-2. Common Disk Usage Commands

Command	Purpose
df -h	Show available disk space (human-readable).
du -h /path	Show space used by specific files/directories.
lsblk	List all block devices (disks, partitions).

Example:

```
$df -h
Filesystem      Size  Used Avail Use% Mounted on
tmpfs           383M  5.1M  378M   2% /run
/dev/sda2       458G   52G  383G  12% /
tmpfs           1.9G   38M  1.9G   2% /dev/shm
tmpfs           5.0M   12K  5.0M   1% /run/lock
tmpfs           383M  108K  382M   1% /run/user/1000
$ lsblk
NAME    MAJ:MIN RM   SIZE RO TYPE MOUNTPOINTS
sda       8:0    0 465.8G  0 disk
├─sda1    8:1    0    1M   0 part
└─sda2    8:2    0 465.8G  0 part /var/snap/firefox/common/host-hunspell
                                  /
sr0      11:0    1  1024M  0 rom
zram0   251:0    0   256M  0 disk
```

Disk Partitioning

Partitioning divides a physical disk into separate sections that can be formatted and mounted independently.

We usually create

- A main filesystem partition (e.g., /mnt/data)
- (Optional) Additional partitions for /boot, /home, etc.

Partitioning a Disk with fdisk

List all disks:

```
$ sudo fdisk -l
Disk /dev/sda: 50 GiB
Disk /dev/sdb: 100 GiB

Device     Boot Start        End   Sectors   Size Type
/dev/sda1       2048  104857599 104855552    50G Linux filesystem
/dev/sdb1       2048  209715199 209713152   100G Linux filesystem
```

Note Always double-check that you're partitioning the correct disk!

Creating a Filesystem Partition on /dev/sdb

Launch fdisk:

```
$ sudo fdisk /dev/sdb
```

Inside the fdisk prompt, follow this sequence:

```
Command (m for help): n       ← Create a new partition
Partition type: p             ← Primary partition
Partition number: 1           ← First partition
First sector: [press Enter]
Last sector: +100G            ← Allocate 100GB

Command (m for help): w       ← Write changes and exit
```

Formatting Partitions

After creating a partition, you need to format it with a filesystem so that the operating system can read and write data from and to it. Different filesystem types are available depending on performance needs, compatibility, and intended use (see Table 3-3).

Table 3-3. *Common Linux Filesystem Types*

Filesystem Type	Purpose
ext4	Most common Linux filesystem
xfs	High-performance filesystem (good for servers)
vfat	Compatible with Windows (USB drives)

Example: Format a partition with ext4:

```
$ sudo mkfs.ext4 /dev/sdb1
mke2fs 1.46.5 (30-Dec-2021)
Creating filesystem with 26214144 4k blocks and 6553600 inodes
Filesystem UUID: b7e4b2e1-4a6b-4879-8171-xxxxxxxxxxxx
Superblock backups stored on blocks:
        32768, 98304, 163840, ...
Allocating group tables: done
Writing inode tables: done
Creating journal (262144 blocks): done
Writing superblocks and filesystem accounting information: done
(Replace /dev/sdb with your disk name.)
```

Mounting and Unmounting Filesystems

Mounting a filesystem means attaching it to a specific directory (called a mount point) so that it becomes accessible to the system. Unmounting detaches the filesystem, making it safe to remove or reconfigure the storage device.

The commands in Table 3-4 are used to manage filesystem mounts in Linux.

Table 3-4. *Commands for Mounting and Unmounting Filesystems*

Command	Purpose
mount	Attach a filesystem to a directory.
umount	Detach a filesystem.

CHAPTER 3 FILESYSTEM MANAGEMENT

Manually Mount a Drive

```
$ sudo mount /dev/sdb1 /mnt
```

Unmount the Drive

```
$ sudo umount /mnt
```

Important Always unmount a disk before removing it!

Making Mounts Permanent with /etc/fstab

If you want Linux to mount a disk automatically at boot, you need to add an entry to the /etc/fstab file.

To edit /etc/fstab:

```
sudo nano /etc/fsta
```

Add a line like this:

```
/dev/sdb1    /mnt    ext4    defaults    0  2
```

Creating and Managing Swap Space

Swap space acts like emergency RAM when your system runs out of memory. It helps prevent crashes by providing extra virtual memory on disk.

Check Current Swap Space

```
$ free -h
              total      used      free    shared  buff/cache   available
Mem:          3.8G       1.2G      1.1G      122M        1.5G        2.3G
Swap:         0B         0B        0B
```

Creating a Swap File

```
$ sudo fallocate -l 2G /swapfile
$ sudo chmod 600 /swapfile
$ sudo mkswap /swapfile
Setting up swapspace version 1, size = 2 GiB (2147483648 bytes)
no label, UUID=xxxxxxxx-xxxx-xxxx-xxxx-xxxxxxxxxxxx
$ sudo swapon /swapfile
To make it permanent, add this line to /etc/fstab:
 /swapfile swap swap defaults 0 0
Confirm:
$ free -h
              total        used        free      shared  buff/cache   available
Mem:           3.8G        1.2G        1.1G        122M        1.5G        2.3G
Swap:          2.0G          0B        2.0G
```

Tuning vm.swappiness

The Linux kernel controls how aggressively it uses swap via the vm.swappiness parameter (default is usually 60). Lower values (e.g., 10) make the system prefer RAM, while higher values make it use swap more readily.

To check the current value:

```
$ cat /proc/sys/vm/swappiness
60
```

To temporarily set it (until reboot):

```
sudo sysctl vm.swappiness=10
```

To make it permanent, add this line to /etc/sysctl.conf:

```
vm.swappiness=10
```

Swap and Hibernation

If you plan to use hibernation (suspend-to-disk), note that a swap file may require extra configuration on some Linux distributions to work correctly, such as specifying the

CHAPTER 3　FILESYSTEM MANAGEMENT

swap device's UUID in the bootloader parameters. Swap partitions are generally more straightforward for hibernation support.

Tip　Swap doesn't replace RAM, but it prevents crashes when memory usage spikes.

Monitoring Disk Health

Keeping your storage healthy is crucial for system reliability.

Check Disk IO Usage

```
$ iostat -x 1 5
Linux 6.11.0-24-generic (master-node)    05/07/2025    _x86_64_    (4 CPU)
avg-cpu:  %user   %nice %system %iowait  %steal   %idle
           8.70    0.07    3.13    5.00    0.00   83.11
Device             r/s     rkB/s    rrqm/s  %rrqm r_await
rareq-sz     w/s     wkB/s    wrqm/s  %wrqm w_await wareq-
sz      d/s     dkB/s    drqm/s  %drqm d_await dareq-sz      f/s f_await  aqu-
sz   %util
sda              18.99    878.60    5.76   23.29   16.42   46.28
18.98    452.84    25.58  57.40   10.17   23.86    0.00    0.00    0.00
0.00    0.00    0.00    1.77   27.24    0.55   10.43
zram0             6.76     27.14    0.00    0.00    0.00    4.02
7.47    29.88    0.00    0.00    0.01    4.00    0.00
0.00    0.00    0.00    0.00    0.00    0.00    0.00    0.00    0.01
(Install sysstat package if needed.)
```

SMART Disk Health Check

Install smart tools:

```
$ sudo apt install smartmontools
```

Run a quick SMART check:

```
$ sudo smartctl -H /dev/sda
smartctl 7.4 2023-08-01 r5530 [x86_64-linux-6.11.0-24-generic]
(local build)
Copyright (C) 2002-23, Bruce Allen, Christian Franke, www.smartmontools.org
=== START OF READ SMART DATA SECTION ===
SMART overall-health self-assessment test result: PASSED
```

Please note the following marginal attributes:

```
ID# ATTRIBUTE_NAME          FLAG     VALUE WORST THRESH TYPE
UPDATED   WHEN_FAILED RAW_VALUE
190 Airflow_Temperature_Cel 0x0022   054   037   045    Old_
age    Always    In_the_past 46 (Min/Max 43/46 #659)
```

Explanation of the command output:

- PASSED: Good
- FAILED: Time to back up and replace!

Key Takeaways

- Linux organizes everything in a single directory tree starting from /.
- You partition disks with `fdisk`, format them with `mkfs`, and mount them with `mount`.
- Swap space acts as backup memory when physical RAM is low, helping to prevent crashes.
- Monitoring disk usage and health is essential to avoid unexpected failures.
- Use tools like `df`, `lsblk`, `iostat`, and `smartctl` to check storage usage and status.

  (Note: Some tools may require installation—e.g., `tree`, `iostat`, `smartctl`.)

- Always use UUID values in /etc/fstab to make mounts persistent and stable.

- Be cautious with destructive disk operations—always verify the target device.

Filesystem management is a core skill for every Linux system administrator. With the tools and techniques covered in this chapter, you're now equipped to handle storage confidently and effectively.

CHAPTER 4

Basic System Configuration

System configuration is at the heart of what makes a Linux server or workstation reliable, secure, and efficient. Once Linux is installed and users are created, it's time to transform that raw installation into a responsive, stable, and network-ready system. Whether you're building a personal workstation, a remote web server, or part of a distributed cloud deployment, the way you configure your system defines how it performs and how well it withstands real-world usage.

In this chapter, we'll take a hands-on, practical approach to configuring essential system elements: services, processes, network, time, locales, and automation. These are the core skills that every Linux user, especially system administrators, should master.

Why System Configuration Matters

A good configuration ensures that your system

- Boots the right services at the right time
- Connects reliably to local and remote networks
- Uses accurate time settings and locale formats
- Remains secure, lean, and ready for work

Managing System Services with systemd

Most modern Linux distributions, including Ubuntu, Debian, Fedora, Arch, and RHEL, use systemd to initialize the system and manage services. It replaces older tools like SysVinit and Upstart, and while some find it controversial, its flexibility and performance have made it the default for most distros.

Understanding systemd Units

systemd manages everything using unit files. These are configuration files that define how to start, stop, and monitor services.

Common Unit Types

- .service: Regular services like nginx or sshd
- .socket: Socket activation (services that start on network requests)
- .target: Groups of services for boot stages
- .timer: Scheduled tasks (like cron alternatives)

Example Services

- sshd.service: OpenSSH daemon for remote access
- nginx.service: Web server
- cron.service: Task scheduler

You can find unit files in

- /etc/systemd/system/ (custom or admin-created)
- /lib/systemd/system/ (default units)

Viewing Service Status

To see if a service is running:

```
$ sudo systemctl status ssh
● ssh.service - OpenBSD Secure Shell server
    Loaded: loaded (/lib/systemd/system/ssh.service; enabled; vendor
   preset: enabled)
    Active: active (running) since Sun 2025-07-27 14:23:10 EAT; 15min ago
      Docs: man:sshd(8)
            man:sshd_config(5)
  Main PID: 1234 (sshd)
     Tasks: 1 (limit: 4567)
```

```
    Memory: 2.5M
       CPU: 35ms
    CGroup: /system.slice/ssh.service
            └─1234 /usr/sbin/sshd -D
```

Note On **Ubuntu**, the SSH service unit is named ssh.service. On some other Linux distributions (like CentOS, Fedora, or Arch), it may be called sshd.service. These are usually aliases referring to the same systemd unit. You can use either

```
$ sudo systemctl status ssh
```

or

```
$ sudo systemctl status sshd
```

Both will generally work, but for consistency with Ubuntu-based systems, we'll use ssh throughout this guide.

Starting the SSH Service (If It Didn't Auto-start)

If the service is inactive, you can manually start it:

```
$ sudo systemctl start ssh
```

No output means the command ran successfully. You can confirm again with status.

Enabling SSH on Boot

To ensure the SSH server starts automatically when the system boots:

```
$ sudo systemctl enable ssh
Synchronizing state of ssh.service with SysV service script with /usr/lib/systemd/systemd-sysv-install.
Executing: /usr/lib/systemd/systemd-sysv-install enable ssh
Created symlink /etc/systemd/system/multi-user.target.wants/ssh.service → /usr/lib/systemd/system/ssh.service.
```

> **Note** While some systems might also mention sshd.service, it typically points to the same unit. For clarity and consistency, this guide refers only to ssh.service, which is the standard systemd unit name on most Debian-based systems.

Once enabled, the SSH server will automatically start after reboots, ensuring continued remote access.

Verifying SSH Connectivity

From another system on the same network (or over the internet, if your ports are forwarded), test your connection:

```
$ ssh user@192.168.1.100
user@192.168.1.100's password:
Welcome to Ubuntu 24.04 LTS (GNU/Linux 6.8.0-25-generic x86_64)
 * Documentation:  https://help.ubuntu.com
 * Management:     https://landscape.canonical.com
 * Support:        https://ubuntu.com/advantage
```

List All Services

To view all units (active, inactive, failed):

```
$ systemctl list-units --all
```

- home.mount
    not-found inactive   dead   >
  proc-fs-nfsd.mount
    loaded   active   mounted   >
  proc-sys-fs-binfmt_misc.mount
    loaded   active   mounted   >
- run-credentials-systemd\x2dresolved.service.mount
    not-found inactive   dead   >
- run-credentials-systemd\x2dsysctl.service.mount
    not-found inactive   dead   >
- run-credentials-systemd\x2dsysusers.service.mount
    not-found inactive   dead   >

- `run-credentials-systemd\x2dtmpfiles\x2dclean.service.mount`
     not-found inactive   dead   >
- `run-credentials-systemd\x2dtmpfiles\x2dsetup.service.mount`
     not-found inactive   dead   >
- `run-credentials-systemd\x2dtmpfiles\x2dsetup\x2ddev.service.mount`
     not-found inactive   dead   >
- `run-credentials-systemd\x2dtmpfiles\x2dsetup\x2ddev\x2dearly.service.mount`
     not-found inactive   dead   >
  `run-rpc_pipefs.mount`
     loaded   active   mounted   >
  `run-user-1000-doc.mount`
     loaded   active   mounted   >
  `run-user-1000-gvfs.mount`
     loaded   active   mounted   >
  `run-user-1000.mount`
     loaded   active   mounted   >
- `snap-firefox-4173.mount`
     loaded   failed   failed   >
- `snap-firmware\x2dupdater-127.mount`
     loaded   failed   failed   >
- `snap-gnome\x2d42\x2d2204-176.mount`
     loaded   failed   failed   >
- `snap-gtk\x2dcommon\x2dthemes-1535.mount`
     loaded   failed   failed   >
- `snap-snap\x2dstore-1124.mount`
     loaded   failed   failed   >
- `snap-snapd-21465.mount`
     loaded   failed   failed   >
- `snap-snapd\x2ddesktop\x2dintegration-157.mount`
     loaded   failed   failed

Check Failed Services

To check all failed services, simply run

```
$ systemctl --failed
```

UNIT	LOAD	ACTIVE	SUB	DESCRIPTION
● snap-firefox-4173.mount	loaded	failed	failed	Mount unit for firefox, revision 4173
● snap-firmware\x2dupdater-127.mount	loaded	failed	failed	Mount unit for firmware-updater, revision 127
● snap-gnome\x2d42\x2d2204-176.mount	loaded	failed	failed	Mount unit for gnome-42-2204, revision 176
● snap-gtk\x2dcommon\x2dthemes-1535.mount	loaded	failed	failed	Mount unit for gtk-common-themes, revision 1535
● snap-snap\x2dstore-1124.mount	loaded	failed	failed	Mount unit for snap-store, revision 1124
● snap-snapd-21465.mount	loaded	failed	failed	Mount unit for snapd, revision 21465
● snap-snapd\x2ddesktop\x2dintegration-157.mount	loaded	failed	failed	Mount unit for snapd-desktop-integration, revision 157
● cyrus-imapd.service	loaded	failed	failed	Cyrus IMAP/POP3 daemons
● fwupd-refresh.service	loaded	failed	failed	Refresh fwupd metadata and update motd
● inn2.service	loaded	failed	failed	InterNetNews
● knockd.service	loaded	failed	failed	Port-Knock Daemon
● minio.service	loaded	failed	failed	MinIO Storage Server
● openipmi.service	loaded	failed	failed	LSB: OpenIPMI Driver init script

Legend: LOAD → Reflects whether the unit definition was properly loaded.

ACTIVE → The high-level unit activation state, i.e.
         generalization of SUB.
SUB   → The low-level unit activation state, values depend on
         unit type.
13 loaded units listed.

Process Management

In Linux, every running application, script, or service is a **process**. Each process has a unique **PID** (Process ID) and consumes system resources like CPU, memory, and I/O.

Managing processes is essential for

- Troubleshooting frozen or misbehaving apps
- Monitoring system performance
- Controlling resource usage
- Automating cleanup and job control

Viewing Running Processes with ps aux

The ps aux command provides a quick, one-time snapshot of all running processes:

```
$ ps aux
```

This shows all processes currently running on the system, along with their resource usage:

```
USER       PID %CPU %MEM    VIRT    RES   SHR S  TIME+   COMMAND
root         1  0.0  0.1    9120   5680  4320 S  00:01.20 systemd
alice     2345  2.3  1.5  944124  65432 12345 S  00:12.34 firefox
alice     2789  0.1  0.2   10416   4128  2000 S  00:00.45 bash
root      1301  0.0  0.0       0      0     0 I  00:00.00
[kworker/0:1-events]
```

> **Note** Output will vary depending on your system. The numbers above are **examples only**.
>
> High VIRT (virtual memory) values are normal on modern Linux systems and **don't necessarily indicate a problem**.

When you run ps aux, top, or htop, you'll see a table of processes with columns like PID, %CPU, VIRT, etc. Table 4-1 explains what these fields mean and why they matter.

Table 4-1. Understanding Common Fields in ps and top

Column	Meaning
PID	Process ID—a unique identifier for each running process.
USER	The user who owns the process.
%CPU	CPU usage percentage—how much CPU time the process is consuming.
%MEM	Memory usage percentage—the portion of system RAM being used.
VIRT	Virtual memory—total memory the process can access, including code, data, and shared libraries. Often large due to memory mapping, but not all is resident in RAM.
RES	Resident memory—the actual physical RAM currently used by the process.
TIME+	Total CPU time the process has used since it started. Format: minutes:seconds.tenths
COMMAND	The command or program that launched the process (and its arguments, if any).

Real-Time Monitoring with top

To view active processes and system resource usage in real time:

$ top

This provides a live, updating display of

- **CPU usage** (user/system/idle)
- **Memory and swap usage**
- **Top resource-consuming processes**
- **Dynamic updates** every few seconds

> **Tip** Use top when you need to **monitor spikes in CPU or RAM usage**, **track runaway processes**, or **troubleshoot performance issues** as they happen.

Enhanced Interactive View with htop

htop is a more user-friendly, interactive alternative to top, offering (see Figure 4-1)

- **Color-coded bars** for CPU, memory, and swap usage—easier to interpret at a glance

- **Search and filter** capabilities (In htop, press the / key to activate the search function. You can then type a process name or PID to quickly locate the desired process in the list)

- **Easy process management**—select a process and press F9 to kill it or send signals

- **Real-time monitoring** with a clean, scrollable interface

    ```
    $ htop
    ```

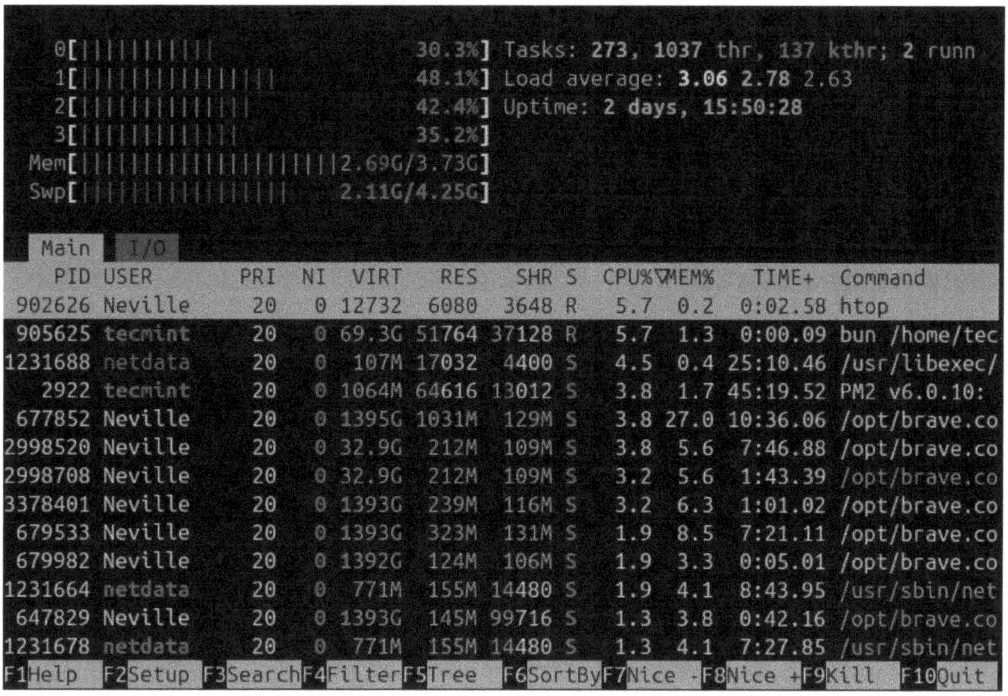

Figure 4-1. htop output showing real-time system resource usage and processes

> **Note** The values and processes shown will differ on your system depending on current activity and hardware.

In addition, if htop is not installed on your system, you can install it using your package manager:

- Debian/Ubuntu: sudo apt install htop
- Red Hat/CentOS/Fedora: sudo dnf install htop
- Arch Linux: sudo pacman -S htop

Table 4-2 summarizes common commands used to monitor system processes, along with typical scenarios where each tool is most effective.

Table 4-2. Use Cases—When to Use Which Tool

Tool	User Case
ps aux	Provides a snapshot of all running processes; useful for scripting or quick, one-time checks
top	Offers real-time monitoring of CPU, memory, and process activity
htop	Provides an interactive interface with easy sorting, filtering, and process management

Managing Processes

Once you've identified a process, you may want to manage it—terminate it, adjust its priority, or control it within your shell. The tools and commands below cover basic process management tasks that every Linux user should know.

Killing a Process

To stop a running process, you first need its **PID** (Process ID).

Find a process by name:

```
ps aux | grep firefox
```

Example output (values will differ on your system):

```
alice      3456   5.4  3.2 944124 65432 ?  Sl    15:00    0:12 firefox
```

Terminate the process:

```
kill 3456
```

Force termination (only if necessary):

```
kill -9 3456
```

Note Use kill -9 (SIGKILL) only as a last resort. It forcibly stops a process without giving it a chance to clean up.

Sending Signals

You can send various signals to a process—not just kill it. Signals instruct the OS how to interact with the process (e.g., terminate gracefully, reload config, or force quit) (see Table 4-3).

Table 4-3. Common Signals You Can Send to Processes

Signal Name	Command Example	Purpose
SIGTERM (15)	kill 3456	Graceful termination (default behavior).
SIGKILL (9)	kill -9 3456	Immediate force-stop (no cleanup).
SIGHUP (1)	kill -1 3456	Reload configuration (used by some daemons).

Tip

- Always try SIGTERM first—it allows the process to shut down cleanly.
- Use SIGKILL only if the process is frozen or unresponsive.
- SIGHUP is useful for reloading services like nginx without restarting them.

Adjusting Process Priority

Linux runs many processes at once. To decide **which gets more CPU time**, the system uses **"priority levels"**—and you can control these using

- nice: To **start** a process with a specific priority
- renice: To **change** the priority of a running process

What Is "nice"?

"nice" is a value from **-20 to 19**:

- A **higher nice value (like 10)** = **lower priority** (your process gets less CPU)
- A **lower value (like -5)** = **higher priority** (your process gets more CPU time)

Start a new process with lower priority:

nice -n 10 ./my_script.sh

This runs my_script.sh with lower priority (so it won't hog the CPU).
Change the priority of a running process:

renice -n 5 -p 3456

This changes the priority of process **PID 3456** to **5** (lower than default).

Note

- The **default priority is 0**.
- **Only root** can assign **negative values** (for higher-than-default priority).
- Use top or htop to view nice values (NI column).

Job Control in the Shell

For tasks launched from a terminal session, Linux supports **job control**, allowing you to pause, resume, and manage background processes.

Run in the background:

```
$ sleep 1000 &
[1] 103814
```

List current jobs:

```
$ jobs
[1]+  Running                 sleep 1000
Bring a job to the foreground:
$ fg %1
```

Send it back to background:

```
$ bg %1
```

Use & and job control when multitasking in the terminal or writing automation scripts.

Basic Networking Setup

Networking is one of the most critical aspects of Linux configuration. If your system can't reach the internet or your local network, many tools, from updates to remote access, stop working.

This section is specific to Ubuntu- and Debian-based systems using **Netplan** (default in Ubuntu 18.04+ and 22.04+).

Other Linux distributions use different network configuration tools:

- Fedora/RHEL/CentOS: Use **NetworkManager** (nmcli) or **systemd-networkd**
- Arch Linux: Often uses **systemd-networkd** or manual interface files

If you're using a non-Debian-based system, refer to your distribution's networking documentation.

CHAPTER 4   BASIC SYSTEM CONFIGURATION

Checking Network Interfaces

To list available network interfaces and their current status:

```
$ ip a

1: lo: <LOOPBACK,UP,LOWER_UP> mtu 65536 qdisc noqueue state UNKNOWN group
default qlen 1000
    link/loopback 00:00:00:00:00:00 brd 00:00:00:00:00:00
    inet 127.0.0.1/8 scope host lo
       valid_lft forever preferred_lft forever
    inet6 ::1/128 scope host noprefixroute
       valid_lft forever preferred_lft forever
2: eno1: <NO-CARRIER,BROADCAST,MULTICAST,UP> mtu 1500 qdisc fq_codel state
DOWN group default qlen 1000
    link/ether 34:e6:d7:16:91:91 brd ff:ff:ff:ff:ff:ff
    altname enp0s25
3: wlp2s0: <BROADCAST,MULTICAST,UP,LOWER_UP> mtu 1500 qdisc noqueue state
UP group default qlen 1000
    link/ether 48:51:b7:2c:24:be brd ff:ff:ff:ff:ff:ff
    inet 192.168.1.11/24 brd 192.168.1.255 scope global dynamic
noprefixroute wlp2s0
       valid_lft 83971sec preferred_lft 83971sec
    inet6 fe80::5613:dd4a:b554:6d12/64 scope link noprefixroute
       valid_lft forever preferred_lft forever
```

Interface breakdown:

- lo: Loopback interface (127.0.0.1), used for internal communications
- eno1: Wired Ethernet interface (inactive: state DOWN)
- wlp2s0: Wi-Fi interface (active: state UP, IP: 192.168.1.11)
- inet: Shows IPv4 address (e.g., 192.168.1.11/24)

> **Important** Your interface names will likely differ (e.g., enp0s3, eth0, ens33).
>
> Always identify the correct name using ip a. Do **not** copy eno1 from the example unless it matches your system.

Setting a Static IP Address (Ubuntu Netplan)

Ubuntu 22.04+ uses **Netplan** to configure network interfaces. Configuration files are stored in /etc/netplan/.

Edit (or create) a configuration file:

```
$ sudo nano /etc/netplan/01-netcfg.yaml
```

Example config:

```
network:
  version: 2
  ethernets:
    eno1:
      dhcp4: no
      addresses:
        - 192.168.1.100/24
      gateway4: 192.168.1.1
      nameservers:
        addresses: [8.8.8.8, 1.1.1.1]
```

YAML is indentation-sensitive. Use spaces (not tabs), and maintain consistent indentation. Misaligned spacing can break your network configuration.

Replace eno1 with your actual interface name (e.g., enp0s3, eth0, ens33)—find it using ip a.

Validating and Applying Netplan Safely

Instead of applying the changes blindly, use the **safe test mode**:

```
$ sudo netplan try
```

CHAPTER 4   BASIC SYSTEM CONFIGURATION

This will

- Apply the configuration temporarily.
- Give you 120 seconds to confirm if it's working.
- Automatically revert if you lose network connectivity or don't confirm.

Once you're sure the config is correct:

```
$ sudo netplan apply
```

For debugging issues:

```
$ sudo netplan --debug apply
```

Netplan files must be stored in /etc/netplan/ and named with a .yaml extension. The filename doesn't matter (e.g., 01-netcfg.yaml, 99-custom.yaml)—only the contents and order do.

Confirming the IP Address

To check the current IP of your interface (e.g., eno1):

```
$ ip a show eno1
2: eno1: <BROADCAST,MULTICAST,UP,LOWER_UP> mtu 1500 ...
    inet 192.168.1.100/24 brd 192.168.1.255 scope global eno1
```

Testing Network Connectivity to the Local Gateway

First, check if your system can reach your local network gateway by pinging its IP address:

```
$ ping -c 3 192.168.1.1

PING 192.168.1.1 (192.168.1.1) 56(84) bytes of data.
64 bytes from 192.168.1.1: icmp_seq=1 ttl=64 time=7.89 ms
64 bytes from 192.168.1.1: icmp_seq=2 ttl=64 time=24.5 ms
```

```
64 bytes from 192.168.1.1: icmp_seq=3 ttl=64 time=2.98 ms
--- 192.168.1.1 ping statistics ---
3 packets transmitted, 3 received, 0% packet loss, time 2002ms
rtt min/avg/max/mdev = 2.979/11.791/24.501/9.208 ms
```

Testing Connectivity to an External Domain

Next, verify internet access by pinging a well-known external domain like google.com:

```
$ ping -c 3 google.com
PING google.com (192.178.54.14) 56(84) bytes of data.
64 bytes from tzjnba-ac-in-f14.1e100.net (192.178.54.14): icmp_seq=1
ttl=114 time=59.0 ms
64 bytes from tzjnba-ac-in-f14.1e100.net (192.178.54.14): icmp_seq=2
ttl=114 time=62.0 ms
64 bytes from tzjnba-ac-in-f14.1e100.net (192.178.54.14): icmp_seq=3
ttl=114 time=60.4 ms
--- google.com ping statistics ---
3 packets transmitted, 3 received, 0% packet loss, time 2003ms
rtt min/avg/max/mdev = 58.974/60.436/61.983/1.229 ms
```

Checking DNS Resolution

Use dig to verify that DNS (Domain Name System) resolution is working correctly by querying a domain name:

```
$ dig openai.com +short
104.18.33.45
172.64.154.211
```

The IP addresses returned may vary depending on your DNS resolver and can change over time due to load balancing or updates.

CHAPTER 4 BASIC SYSTEM CONFIGURATION

System Time and Time Zone Configuration

Accurate system time is critical—not just for logs, but also for scheduled jobs (like cron), certificate validity, and file timestamps. Ensuring your system has the correct time zone and time configuration helps avoid unnecessary issues.

Setting the Time Zone

To list available time zones on your system, run

```
$ timedatectl list-timezones
Africa/Abidjan
Africa/Accra
Africa/Addis_Ababa
Africa/Algiers
Africa/Asmara
Africa/Asmera
Africa/Bamako
Africa/Bangui
Africa/Banjul
Africa/Bissau
Africa/Blantyre
Africa/Brazzaville
Africa/Bujumbura
Africa/Cairo
Africa/Casablanca
Africa/Ceuta
Africa/Conakry
Africa/Dakar
Africa/Dar_es_Salaam
Africa/Djibouti
Africa/Douala
Africa/El_Aaiun
Africa/Freetown
Africa/Gaborone
Africa/Harare
```

```
Africa/Johannesburg
Africa/Juba
Africa/Kampala
Africa/Khartoum
Africa/Kigali
------
```

> **Tip** Time zone strings are case-sensitive. Make sure to use the exact name from the list (e.g., Africa/Nairobi, not africa/nairobi or Africa/nairobi).

Set Your Time Zone

To set the system time zone, use

```
$ sudo timedatectl set-timezone Africa/Nairobi
```

Replace Africa/Nairobi with the correct time zone string from the list.

Synchronizing Time with NTP or Chrony

Modern Linux systems typically use systemd-timesyncd for time synchronization. However, other options are available, especially when you need more precision or flexibility:

- ntp: Older but stable and widely used
- chrony: Recommended; faster synchronization and particularly well-suited for virtual machines

Install Chrony (Recommended)

To install chrony on Debian-based systems:

```
$ sudo apt install chrony
```

apt vs. apt-get in Scripts

While apt is the preferred command-line interface for users due to its cleaner output and progress bars, **apt-get is recommended for scripts**. Here's why:

- apt is designed for interactive use and may change behavior over time.
- apt-get is more stable and predictable in automation.

To avoid prompts during installation or upgrades in scripts, use

```
$ sudo DEBIAN_FRONTEND=noninteractive apt-get -y install chrony
```

This suppresses interactive prompts, ensuring the script continues without pausing.

Tip Avoid using apt in scripts to reduce the risk of unexpected behavior during upgrades or installs. apt-get and apt-key are better suited for automation.

Check Sync Status

```
$ timedatectl status
              Local time: Mon 2025-07-28 19:58:14 EAT
          Universal time: Mon 2025-07-28 16:58:14 UTC
                RTC time: Mon 2025-07-28 16:58:14
               Time zone: Africa/Nairobi (EAT, +0300)
System clock synchronized: yes
             NTP service: active
         RTC in local TZ: no
```

Hardware Clock vs. System Clock

Check hardware clock:

```
$ sudo hwclock --show
2025-07-28 19:59:09.276536+03:00
```

Sync system time to hardware:

```
$ sudo hwclock --systohc
```

Or sync hardware to system:

```
$ sudo hwclock --hctosys
```

Locale and Language Settings

Locales control how the system handles language, currency, date/time formats, and character encoding.

Viewing the Current Locale

```
$ locale
LANG=en_US.UTF-8
LANGUAGE=
LC_CTYPE="en_US.UTF-8"
LC_NUMERIC="en_US.UTF-8"
LC_TIME="en_US.UTF-8"
LC_COLLATE="en_US.UTF-8"
LC_MONETARY="en_US.UTF-8"
LC_MESSAGES="en_US.UTF-8"
LC_PAPER="en_US.UTF-8"
LC_NAME="en_US.UTF-8"
LC_ADDRESS="en_US.UTF-8"
LC_TELEPHONE="en_US.UTF-8"
LC_MEASUREMENT="en_US.UTF-8"
LC_IDENTIFICATION="en_US.UTF-8"
LC_ALL=
```

Generate a new locale (see Figure 4-2):

```
$ sudo dpkg-reconfigure locales
```

CHAPTER 4 BASIC SYSTEM CONFIGURATION

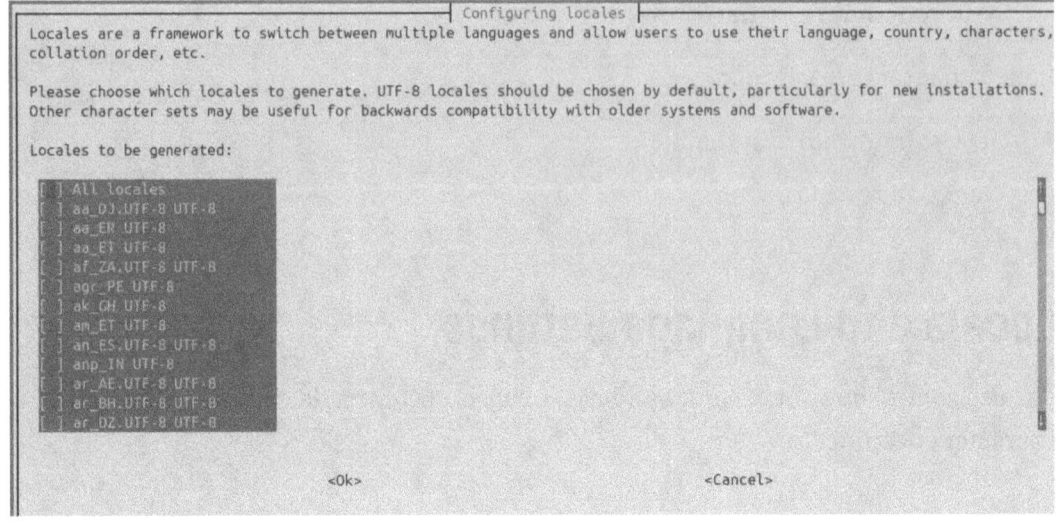

Figure 4-2. *Configuration screen for setting system locales. The interface displays a list of available locales.*

Common options:

- en_US.UTF-8: Universal English
- fr_FR.UTF-8: French
- ja_JP.UTF-8: Japanese

Setting the Default Language

Edit /etc/default/locale:

```
$ echo 'LANG=en_US.UTF-8' | sudo tee /etc/default/locale
```

Or user-specific (in ~/.bashrc):

```
$ echo 'export LANG=en_US.UTF-8' >> ~/.bashrc
```

Verify:

```
$ source ~/.bashrc
$ locale
```

Automating Configuration with Scripts

Once you've configured one system, you probably don't want to repeat everything manually. This is where automation helps—setup scripts can handle repetitive tasks efficiently and consistently.

Example setup script:

```
#!/bin/bash

# Exit immediately on error
set -e

# Update packages
apt update && apt upgrade -y

# Install base tools
apt install -y curl git vim ufw htop

# Set timezone
timedatectl set-timezone Africa/Nairobi

# Enable firewall (non-interactive)
ufw allow OpenSSH
ufw --force enable

# Create a user (interactive login or SSH key preferred)
useradd -m -s /bin/bash devops
chage -d 0 devops  # Force password change on first login

# Enable and start SSH service
systemctl enable ssh
systemctl start ssh
```

Save as setup.sh and exit.

Make the script executable and then run it:

```
$ chmod +x setup.sh
$ sudo ./setup.sh
```

CHAPTER 4 BASIC SYSTEM CONFIGURATION

Output example:

```
Hit:12 http://ke.archive.ubuntu.com/ubuntu noble-backports InRelease
...
Setting time zone to Africa/Nairobi
Firewall enabled: allowing OpenSSH
Creating new user devops...
Adding password for user devops
...
```

Notes on Automation

Avoid hardcoded passwords. The following is not recommended:

```
echo "devops:password" | chpasswd   # ✗ Insecure
```

Hardcoding passwords is insecure and should be avoided. Instead:

- Use chage -d 0 devops to force the user to set a new password at first login.
- For SSH-based access, create the user and add an SSH key to ~devops/.ssh/authorized_keys.
- If you must set a password in automation, read it from a **secure vault** or **environment variable**, and ensure the script is not stored in a public or insecure location.

Non-interactive UFW (Uncomplicated Firewall) Setup

By default, ufw enable prompts for confirmation, which can **cause scripts to hang**.
Use one of the following in non-interactive scripts:

```
ufw --force enable
# or
yes | ufw enable
```

Conclusion

System configuration may seem tedious at first, but it's the bedrock of any functioning Linux environment. Whether you're automating server setups, prepping your machine for software development, or securing a multi-user system, these foundational tasks are where your sysadmin journey truly begins.

In the next chapter, we'll dive into package management, installing, updating, and maintaining the software you need to build out your systems effectively.

CHAPTER 5

Package Management

Managing software on a Linux system is one of the most critical and frequent tasks for both system administrators and developers. Whether you're setting up a new application, applying security updates, or removing unnecessary packages, effective package management ensures your system remains secure, efficient, and maintainable.

In this chapter, we'll cover

- **Fundamentals of package management**
- **Classic tools:** APT (Advanced Package Tool), DNF (Dandified YUM)/YUM, RPM, Pacman
- **Emerging systems:** Nix, Guix, Flatpak, Snap
- **GUI and web-based tools**
- **Security, best practices, and audit recommendations**

Understanding Package Management

Linux distributions provide a rich variety of package management systems, each aligned with the philosophy and technical goals of its ecosystem. These tools automate software installation, upgrading, configuration, and removal—working with a range of package types, from compiled binaries to source-based builds.

To help navigate this landscape, Table 5-1 gives a comparative overview of common systems, formats, and core package tools.

Table 5-1. Package Management Tools by System

System	Format	Tools
Debian-based	.deb	apt, dpkg
Red Hat–based	.rpm	dnf, yum (legacy), rpm
Arch-based	.pkg.tar.zst	pacman (official repos only)
NixOS/other Linux	store path	nix, nix profile install, nixos-rebuild
Guix System	Guile-based	guix, guix system
Gentoo-based	source builds	emerge, portage
Slackware-based	.tgz, .txz	slackpkg, pkgtool
Void Linux	.xbps	xbps-install, xbps-query, xbps-remove
Solus	.eopkg	eopkg
CRUX	source builds	pkgmk, pkgadd, prt-get

Note on Arch and the AUR: pacman manages official repository packages. The Arch User Repository (AUR) is a separate, community-driven source that requires helper tools such as yay or paru or manual PKGBUILD compilation. It is not directly supported by pacman.

Note on Nix: The nix-env tool is still available but considered legacy for many workflows. Modern usage favors declarative installs such as

```
$ nix profile install nixpkgs#htop
```

or, in Flakes-enabled environments,

```
$ nix run nixpkgs#htop
```

Placeholder and Example Policy

Throughout this chapter, example commands and outputs are used to illustrate concepts. To avoid confusion:

- We use **<version>** or **<package-name>** as placeholders (e.g., nginx-<version>.rpm).

- Where applicable, **realistic examples** with valid version numbers or URLs are used.
- All outputs are either taken from actual command runs or clearly marked as illustrative.

This distinction helps prevent confusion between real system behavior and explanatory snippets.

Universal Package Management Wrappers

Many GUI and cross-distribution tools rely on abstraction layers that provide a consistent package management experience across systems.

- PackageKit: Offers a DBus-based API that abstracts underlying package managers such as APT, DNF/YUM, and Zypper. It powers GUI tools like GNOME Software and KDE Discover.
- AppStream: Supplies structured metadata (descriptions, screenshots, categories) for applications. This enables rich, searchable user interfaces in software centers across desktop environments.

These systems help unify application discovery, installation, and updates, even across diverse packaging backends.

APT/dpkg (Debian, Ubuntu, Linux Mint)

APT (Advanced Package Tool) is the primary package management system for Debian-based Linux distributions such as

- Ubuntu 25.04 ("Plucky Puffin")
- Debian 13
- Linux Mint 22

APT serves as a high-level interface to the dpkg package system. It automates package installs, dependency resolution, updates, and cleanup while providing powerful tools for system management. Its design emphasizes stability and ease of use, making it a favorite among both desktop users and system administrators.

APT is often integrated with tools like

- apt-mark for package pinning and holding
- unattended-upgrades for automatic security updates
- Graphical tools like **Synaptic Package Manager** or **GNOME Software**

APT Command Examples (Ubuntu 25.04)

The following sections presents some APT commands and their outputs.

> **Note** The output below is based on Ubuntu 25.04 (Plucky Puffin).

Update Package Lists

```
$ sudo apt update
Hit:1 http://archive.ubuntu.com/ubuntu plucky InRelease
Reading package lists... Done
Building dependency tree
Reading state information... Done
```

Install Packages

```
$ sudo apt install nginx -y
Reading package lists... Done
Building dependency tree
Reading state information... Done
```

The following *new* packages will be installed:

```
nginx libnginx-mod-http-image-filter libtiff5
```

Upgrade All Packages

```
$ sudo apt upgrade -y
Reading package lists... Done
Calculating upgrade... Done
```

CHAPTER 5 PACKAGE MANAGEMENT

The following packages will be upgraded:

```
openssl (3.4.1-1ubuntu25.04) nginx-core (1.26.3-2ubuntu1.2)
2 upgraded, 0 newly installed, 0 to remove.
Fetched 5,678 kB, freed 1,234 kB
```

Search for a Package

```
$ apt search python3
Python 3.13.3
```

Remove and Purge

```
$ sudo apt remove nginx
```

The following packages will be *removed*:

```
nginx nginx-common nginx-core
$ sudo apt purge nginx
Reading package lists… Done
Building dependency tree
Reading state information… Done
```

The following packages will be *purged*:

```
nginx-core* nginx* nginx-common*
```

Clean Up Packages

```
$ sudo apt autoremove -y
Reading package lists… Done
Building dependency tree
Reading state information… Done
0 to upgrade, 0 to newly install, 3 to remove.
```

After this operation, 12.3 MB disk space will be freed.

Fix Broken Installs

```
$ sudo apt --fix-broken install
Reading package lists... Done
Building dependency tree
Reading state information... Done
Correcting dependencies... Done
0 to install, 0 to remove, 0 not upgraded.
```

> **Note** Version numbers and outputs will differ between releases. You can substitute Ubuntu 25.04 with your current version, such as focal (20.04) or jammy (22.04), as appropriate.

DNF/YUM/RPM (Fedora, RHEL, CentOS, AlmaLinux, Rocky Linux)

DNF (Dandified YUM) is the modern package manager for RPM-based distributions, including Fedora 40, RHEL 9.x, AlmaLinux 9, and Rocky Linux 9. DNF replaced the older **YUM** tool starting with RHEL 8 and Fedora 22+. While the yum command still exists on many systems, it is now simply a **compatibility symlink to DNF**—meaning DNF is the actual backend used in both cases. YUM is no longer maintained as a separate tool and should not be used as if it were distinct from DNF.

DNF offers better performance, enhanced dependency resolution, and a powerful plugin system. It works with .rpm packages and integrates seamlessly with modular repositories, third-party sources, and automation tooling. Whether you're installing packages, locking versions, or automating security updates, DNF provides a scriptable and reliable interface for modern RPM-based Linux distributions.

Below are some DNF command examples and their respective outputs.

Update Repositories

```
$ sudo dnf check-update
Last metadata expiration check: 1:00:00 ago on Tue Apr 15 10:00:00 2025.
...
openssl-3.4.1-1.fc42.x86_64    fedora           3.4.1-1.fc42    updates
```

Install Packages

```
$ sudo dnf install httpd
Dependencies resolved.
================================================================================
 Package         Arch      Version           Repository                   Size
================================================================================
Installing:
 httpd           x86_64    2.4.57-2.fc37     fedora-cisco-openh264        2.9 MB
...
```

Update the System

```
$ sudo dnf upgrade -y
Last metadata expiration check: 0:34:12 ago on ...
Dependencies resolved.
================================================================
 Package    Arch      Version          Repository        Size
================================================================
Upgrading:
 openssl    x86_64    3.0.8-1.fc37     updates           1.2 MB
```

Remove Packages

```
$ sudo dnf remove httpd
Dependencies resolved.
```

```
=============================================================================
 Package            Arch     Version            Repository
=============================================================================
Removing:
 httpd              x86_64   2.4.57-2.fc37      @fedora
Transaction Summary
=============================================================================
Remove 1 Package
```

Clean Metadata

```
$ sudo dnf clean all
34 files removed
```

Auto-remove Unused Dependencies

```
$ sudo dnf autoremove -y
Last metadata expiration check: 0:05:12 ago on Tue Apr 15 12:00:00 2025.
Dependencies resolved.
=============================================================================
Removing:
  some-unused-lib.x86_64   1.2-3.fc42    @updates    150 k
  orphan-tool.noarch       5.4-1.fc42    @fedora      80 k
Transaction Summary
=============================================================================
Remove 2 Packages
Freed space: 230 k
```

Search for Packages

```
$ dnf search nodejs
Last metadata expiration check: 0:05:12 ago on Tue Apr 15 12:00:00 2025.
=========================== Name Exact Matched: nodejs ===========================
nodejs.x86_64 : JavaScript runtime built on Chrome's V8 engine
```

```
nodejs-doc.noarch : Documentation for nodejs
nodejs-minimal.x86_64 : Node.js minimal install
```

Add and Manage Third-Party Repositories (MySQL Example)

To enable third-party repositories like **MySQL**, use the dnf config-manager tool. However, MySQL's repository URLs and naming conventions (e.g., mysql80, mysql84, etc.) **may change over time**, so it's best to always refer to the official MySQL download page to get the current and correct RPM package URL for your system.

Example:

1. Visit the MySQL Yum Repository page: https://dev.mysql.com/downloads/repo/yum/.

2. Copy the appropriate .rpm link for your OS version (e.g., EL8, EL9).

3. Use that URL with the --add-repo command:

   ```
   $ sudo dnf config-manager --add-repo=https://dev.mysql.com/get/mysql84-community-release-el8.rpm
   ```

   Add the repo from https://dev.mysql.com/get/mysql84-community-release-el8.rpm.

Note Don't hardcode the repo name (e.g., mysql80) in scripts or documentation. MySQL periodically updates these names, so always fetch the latest from dev.mysql.com.

Disable and Enable Repos

You can disable or enable a specific repo (such as mysql84-community) as needed:

```
$ sudo dnf config-manager --set-disabled mysql80-community
$ sudo dnf config-manager --set-enabled mysql80-community
```

Pacman (Arch-Based Systems: Arch, Manjaro)

Pacman is the lightweight and powerful package manager used by Arch Linux, Manjaro, and other Arch-based distributions. Designed for speed and simplicity, Pacman utilizes a binary package format and a straightforward command syntax to manage software installation, removal, and upgrades.

Pacman handles **official repositories only** (like core, extra, and community). Access to the **Arch User Repository (AUR)** requires separate AUR helpers such as yay, paru, or manual building of PKGBUILDs. Pacman itself does **not** sync or manage packages from the AUR.

Unlike some package managers, Pacman places users in close control of their system's state and does not abstract away complexity, making it a favorite among power users. However, this requires users to carefully manage partial upgrades, dependency conflicts, and package caching.

Sync and Update

```
$ sudo pacman -Syu
:: Synchronizing package databases…
 core is up to date
 extra is up to date
 community is up to date
resolving dependencies…
looking for conflicting packages…
:: Proceed with installation? [Y/n]
```

Install Packages

```
$ sudo pacman -S htop
resolving dependencies…
looking for conflicting packages…
Packages (1) htop-3.2.1-1
Total Download Size: 132.45 KiB
```

Remove Packages

```
$ sudo pacman -R nginx
checking dependencies...
error: failed to prepare transaction (could not satisfy dependencies)
:: nginx: removing nginx breaks dependency 'nginx'
```

If you want to safely remove a package **along with its dependencies** that are no longer needed by other packages, use

```
$ sudo pacman -Rs nginx
```

This ensures dependencies are removed properly without breaking your system.

Force Remove Without Dependency Checks

```
$ sudo pacman -Rdd nginx
checking dependencies...
warning: removing 'nginx' breaks dependency 'nginx'
:: Starting Force Removal...
removing nginx (1:2.4.2-1)
```

Warning The -Rdd option **bypasses all dependency checks** and can leave your system in an unstable or broken state. Use this only as a last resort and with caution.

Clean Package Cache

```
$ sudo pacman -Sc
Cache directory: /var/cache/pacman/pkg/
Removable packages:
   firefox-150.0-1-x86_64.pkg.tar.zst
   python-3.13.5-2-x86_64.pkg.tar.zst
Proceed? [Y/n] y
```

Search for Packages

```
$ pacman -Ss python
extra/python 3.11.12-1 [installed]
    Interpreted, interactive, object-oriented programming language
extra/python-doc 3.11.12-1
    Documentation for python
community/python-pip 23.2.1-1
```

Nix and Guix: Declarative, Atomic Package Management

Nix and Guix represent a fundamentally different approach to package management compared with traditional tools like APT, DNF, or Pacman. Built around the principles of functional programming, both systems enable declarative, reproducible, and atomic package management. Every installed package exists in an isolated store path, and changes to your system can be rolled back safely thanks to generations.

Nix is widely used on NixOS and also supports other Linux distributions via nix-env. Guix, based on similar principles but built on GNU tooling, powers the GNU Guix System. Both are ideal for CI/CD, research computing, and production environments where immutability, rollback, and reproducibility are critical.

Below are a sample of command outputs and workflows for Nix and Guix.

Nix

Install Packages

Legacy method (still available):

```
$ nix-env -i firefox
installing 'firefox-121.0'
```

These paths will be fetched (25.3 MiB download, 127.6 MiB unpacked):

```
  /nix/store/...
building '/nix/store/...-firefox.drv'...
```

CHAPTER 5 PACKAGE MANAGEMENT

Modern recommended method (Nix 2.12+):

```
$ nix profile install nixpkgs#firefox
```

This uses the new **nix profile** commands, which are designed to replace nix-env workflows, providing clearer and more reproducible package management.

List Installed Packages

```
$ nix-env -q
firefox-138.0
```

Modern:

```
$ nix profile list
```

This lists installed profiles and packages managed by the modern CLI.

Upgrade Packages

```
$ nix-env -u
upgrading 'firefox-137.0' to 'firefox-138.0'
2 package(s) updated, 3 removed
```

Warning   firefox-beta replaced with firefox.

Modern:

```
$ nix profile upgrade
```

Revert to Previous Generation

```
$ nix-env --rollback
```

Switches to the previous profile generation to undo changes safely.

> **Note** The nix-env commands remain available for backward compatibility and legacy workflows but are considered superseded by the new nix profile CLI introduced in Nix 2.12 and later. For new projects and up-to-date workflows, use the modern nix profile commands for more reliable and declarative package management.

Guix (GNU Guix System)

GNU Guix is a functional package manager built on GNU/Linux principles, emphasizing **declarative, reproducible, and transactional** package management. Like Nix, Guix installs packages in isolated store paths, supports atomic upgrades and rollbacks, and allows multiple versions of packages to coexist without conflicts.

Guix is the core package manager for the GNU Guix System but can also be used on other Linux distributions. It prioritizes user freedom, reproducibility, and system rollback capabilities, making it ideal for users who want fine-grained control over their software environments.

Common Guix Commands

Install Packages

```
$ guix install emacs
===> Installing 1/1: emacs-30.1
Downloading 28.0 MiB and building…
```

> **Tip** Before installing or upgrading packages, it's often recommended to run guix pull to update your local channels to the latest package definitions:
>
> ```
> $ guix pull
> ```

This ensures you have the newest package versions and improvements.

List Installed Packages

```
$ guix package --list-installed
emacs              30.1    out    /gnu/store/...-emacs-30.1
coreutils          9.3     out    /gnu/store/...-coreutils-9.3
```

Garbage-Collect Unused Store Items

```
$ guix gc
33 store item(s) deleted, freeing 1.2 GiB
```

Roll Back the Last Transaction

```
$ guix package --roll-back
rolled back profile to generation 3
```

Snap and Flatpak: Containerized Desktop Packaging

Snap and Flatpak provide sandboxed, self-contained environments to run desktop applications on Linux. By isolating dependencies from the system package manager, they allow apps to run consistently across distributions, enable automatic updates, and reduce packaging complexity.

These formats are especially popular for delivering productivity tools, browsers, multimedia apps, and other desktop software without the need to worry about shared library compatibility or distribution-specific packaging quirks.

Snap

Snap is developed and maintained by Canonical, the company behind Ubuntu. Snap packages rely on the Snap Store infrastructure, which centralizes distribution and update management. This has benefits like easy discovery and automatic updates but also creates some reliance on Canonical's ecosystem.

Install Packages

```
$ sudo snap install code --classic
Visual Studio Code 1.100.0 from 'vscode' installed
```

This installs Visual Studio Code version 1.100 with automatic updates from the Snap Store.

The --classic flag grants broader system access, required by IDEs and development tools for full functionality.

Security note Using --classic weakens sandbox isolation by allowing access to most system resources. Use it only if necessary.

List Packages

```
$ snap list

Name    Version    Rev    Tracking       Publisher    Notes
code    1.100.0    2345   latest/stable  vscode*      classic
```

Remove Packages

```
$ sudo snap remove code
code removed
```

Flatpak

Flatpak is a community-driven framework with governance distributed across multiple contributors. It primarily uses Flathub as its main application repository but allows additional remotes.

Install Packages

```
$ flatpak install flathub org.mozilla.firefox
org.mozilla.firefox permissions:
    ipc    network    filesystem    dbus
Is this okay [y/N]? y
Installing in system: org.mozilla.firefox/x86_64/stable from flathub
```

List Packages

```
$ flatpak list
```

```
Name                    Application ID              Version Branch
Installation
Firefox                 org.mozilla.firefox         136.0   stable system
```

Uninstall Packages

```
$ flatpak uninstall org.mozilla.firefox
```

Uninstalled: org.mozilla.firefox

Note Flatpak apps run in a sandbox with strict permission controls. Permissions can be overridden or granted explicitly using command-line options (e.g., --filesystem=home).

Granting broad access such as full home directory access (--filesystem=home) compromises the sandbox's security model. It's strongly recommended to grant only the minimal necessary access, for example, a specific folder like your Documents directory (--filesystem=~/Documents), to maintain better isolation and security.

Slackware-Based Systems (pkgtool/slackpkg, .tgz/.txz)

Slackware is the oldest actively maintained Linux distribution, known for its simplicity, transparency, and adherence to UNIX principles. It avoids abstraction layers and automates very little, favoring manual configuration and giving users full control over their systems. This philosophy extends to its package management system, which is intentionally minimalistic.

Slackware packages use the .tgz or .txz format—compressed tar archives containing precompiled binaries and install scripts. These packages **do not include dependency metadata**, meaning **Slackware does not perform automatic dependency resolution**. You are expected to manually track and install dependencies.

Slackware uses two main tools for package management:

- pkgtool: A menu-driven, local package manager for installing, removing, or upgrading .tgz/.txz packages.
- slackpkg: A command-line wrapper for managing official Slackware packages over the network. It simplifies upgrades and package installation but still assumes you understand and manage dependencies yourself.

Example package management flow (Slackware 15.x):

Initialize and update the package list:

```
$ slackpkg update gpg $ slackpkg update
```

Install any newly added packages:

```
$ slackpkg install-new
```

Upgrade all installed packages:

```
$ slackpkg upgrade-all
```

Remove obsolete packages no longer in the current release:

```
$ slackpkg clean-system
```

Search, install, and remove packages:

```
$ slackpkg search mc
$ slackpkg install mc
$ slackpkg remove vim
```

Important Considerations

Unlike modern package managers like apt, dnf, or pacman, **Slackware does not automatically resolve or install dependencies**. For example, if you're installing a program that depends on a specific library, you'll need to

1. Identify the missing dependency (from documentation or trial-and-error).
2. Download and install it manually using installpkg, pkgtool, or slackpkg.

Example: Manually Installing a Dependency

If you're building or installing an application that requires libfoo, you must

Search for the required package (if available in repos):

```
$ slackpkg search libfoo
```

If not found, manually download or build it:

```
$ installpkg libfoo-1.0.0-x86_64-1.txz
```

Extending Slackware with Community Tools

To make Slackware more flexible and user-friendly, you can adopt community-supported tools:

- slackpkg+: An extension to slackpkg that adds support for third-party and unofficial repositories (e.g., AlienBob, SlackBuilds.org (SBo)). It allows package priorities and multiple repositories, bridging the gap between Slackware's simplicity and modern package convenience.
- **sbopkg**: A curses-based front end to SlackBuilds.org (SBo), providing access to hundreds of user-contributed build scripts for compiling software from source. Automates downloading source code, checking dependencies (informational only), and building packages.

These tools help make Slackware more usable for day-to-day work while respecting its core design philosophy.

Void Linux (XBPS, .xbps)

Void Linux is a minimalist, independent rolling-release distro built from scratch, featuring the XBPS package manager and runit init system. Packages are .xbps, with both binaries and a clean source build system (xbps-src).

Typical xbps commands:

```
$ sudo xbps-install -Suv
$ xbps-query -Rs firefox
$ sudo xbps-install firefox
$ sudo xbps-remove firefox
$ xbps-query -l
```

XBPS automatically tracks dependencies and marks packages as manual or automatic.

Solus (eopkg, .eopkg)

Solus is an independent, curated rolling-release distribution known for the Budgie desktop. Its package manager eopkg (derived from Pardus's PiSi) handles installation, upgrades, removals, and searching with ease. Solus aims for simplicity and usability, optimized for desktop use.

Common eopkg commands:

```
$ sudo eopkg search firefox
$ sudo eopkg install firefox
$ sudo eopkg upgrade
$ sudo eopkg upgrade firefox
$ sudo eopkg remove firefox
$ sudo eopkg info firefox
```

Note Despite its straightforward design, eopkg has a more limited package selection than AUR or Debian repos, which some users offset with Flatpak or third-party repositories.

CRUX (pkgmk, pkgadd, .tar.gz)

CRUX is a lightweight, source-based distribution that emphasizes simplicity and code transparency. It uses pkgmk and pkgadd/pkgdel/pkginfo tools to build and manage packages from source.

Example flow:

```
$ pkgmk -o package-name
$ pkgadd -u package-name.pkg.tar.gz
$ pkgdel package-name
```

Note pkgadd -u will upgrade or reinstall, and configuration rules in /etc/pkgadd.conf help preserve your settings during upgrades.

GUI and Web-Based Tools for Package Management

While command-line tools offer full control, many Linux distributions support graphical and web-based interfaces that simplify package management. These tools are especially helpful for new users, system administrators managing remote machines, and anyone who prefers a visual overview of installed or available packages.

The tools below focus specifically on software/package management. Some are built atop lower-level tools like APT or Pacman, while others offer remote access via the web.

Synaptic Package Manager (Debian, Ubuntu, Linux Mint)

Synaptic is a GTK-based graphical front end for the **APT** package management system. Long regarded as one of the most powerful and reliable GUI package managers on Debian-based systems, it offers a comprehensive view and control over package operations without requiring command-line interaction.

However, while still available and fully functional, **Synaptic is no longer the default GUI package manager** on many modern distributions. Systems like Ubuntu now favor user-friendly "app store" interfaces such as **GNOME Software** or **Ubuntu Software Center**, which are designed for casual users and support additional formats like **Snap** and **Flatpak**.

Despite this, Synaptic remains a **valuable tool for intermediate and advanced users** who need fine-grained package management capabilities that newer GUI tools often abstract away or do not expose.

Key Features

- Browse, search, install, and remove .deb packages.
- Upgrade specific packages or the entire system.
- View package details, changelogs, file lists, and dependency trees.
- Lock packages to a specific version to prevent automatic updates.
- Clean up residual config files and resolve broken installs.
- Queue and batch-process multiple operations efficiently.

Example: Locking a Package Version Using Synaptic

To prevent a package (e.g., Firefox) from being automatically upgraded:

1. Open Synaptic.
2. Search for Firefox.
3. Right-click the package ➤ **Package** ➤ **Lock Version**.

This ensures the selected version stays fixed, which is useful if a newer release causes problems or breaks compatibility (See Figure 5-1).

CHAPTER 5 PACKAGE MANAGEMENT

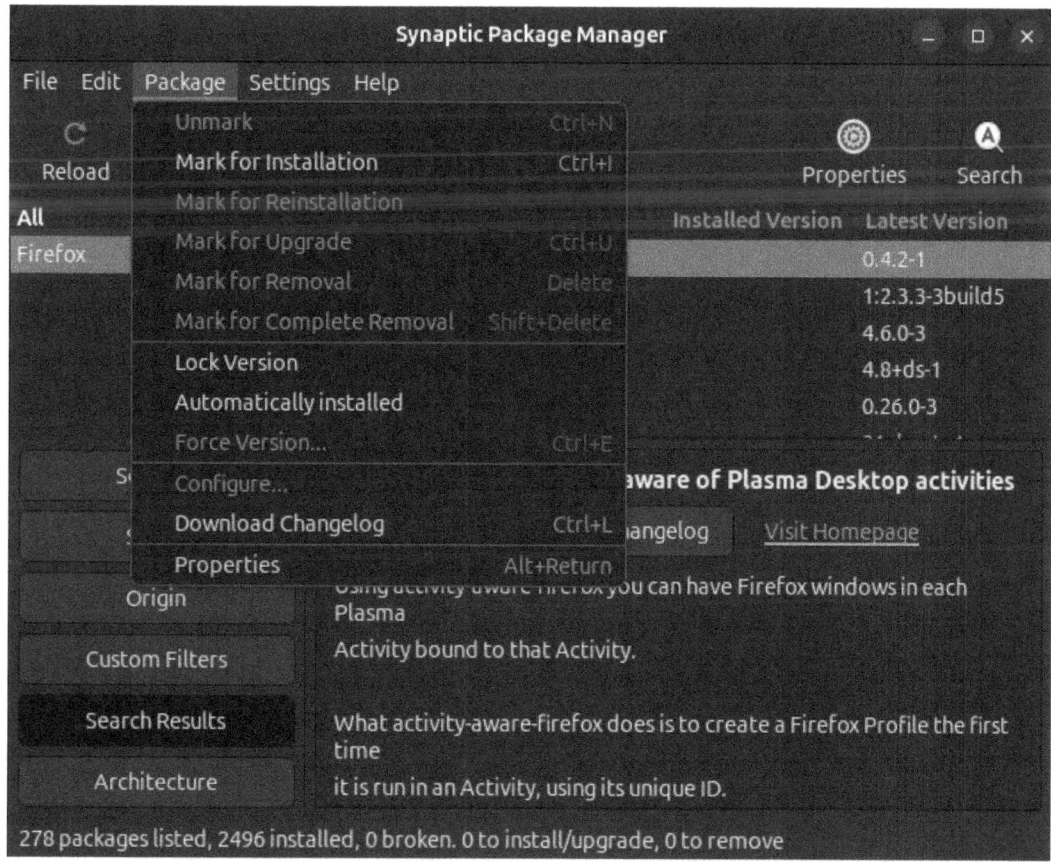

Figure 5-1. Locking Firefox using Synaptic

Limitations

While powerful, Synaptic has notable drawbacks in modern desktop environments:

- Dated interface: It prioritizes function over aesthetics and may feel out of place on modern desktops

- No Snap/Flatpak integration: It only manages .deb packages via APT; Snap and Flatpak packages are not visible or controllable through Synaptic.

- Reduced visibility: It's no longer pre-installed on many Debian-based distros and not promoted to casual users.

Recommended Usage

- Best for: Intermediate to advanced users, system administrators, or those troubleshooting complex dependency issues
- Not ideal for: Casual users looking for a simplified, app store–like experience (they may prefer GNOME Software or Ubuntu Software)

Installation command:

```
$ sudo apt install synaptic
```

Pamac (Manjaro, Arch Linux)

Pamac is a graphical package manager designed for Arch-based systems, especially Manjaro Linux. It integrates with Pacman, the AUR (Arch User Repository), and optionally with Flatpak and Snap, offering a unified interface for package management.

Key Features

- Install, remove, and update software with ease.
- Support for the AUR, Flatpak, and Snap with toggles.
- Clean and modern interface with package history.
- Dependency tree viewer.
- Update notifications and system tray integration.

Perfect for Manjaro users who prefer not to use Pacman or the command line. Great for managing third-party packages (like AUR).

Install via the terminal on Manjaro:

```
$ sudo pacman -S pamac-gtk
```

Cockpit's PackageKit Plugin (Fedora, RHEL, AlmaLinux, Rocky Linux)

Cockpit is a powerful, web-based management interface for Linux servers, designed to simplify common administrative tasks via a modern browser interface. When extended with the PackageKit plugin, Cockpit enables remote package management—installing, updating, and removing software—without needing terminal access or a graphical desktop environment.

This makes it especially well-suited for managing **headless or remote servers**, particularly in enterprise or cloud environments using **Fedora, RHEL, AlmaLinux, or Rocky Linux**.

Key Features

- Browser-based access: Manage your system from https://yourserver:9090.
- Remote updates: View and apply software updates from any device.
- Install/remove packages: Add or remove RPM-based packages via the web UI.
- Real-time monitoring: Track system resource usage and ongoing package operations.
- No GUI required: Works on headless servers without a desktop environment.

Installation and Setup (Fedora/RHEL-Based Systems)

Install Cockpit and the PackageKit Plugin

```
$ sudo dnf install cockpit cockpit-packagekit
```

Enable and Start the Cockpit Web Service

```
$ sudo systemctl enable --now cockpit.socket
```

Once started, Cockpit becomes available at:

```
https://your-server-ip:9090
```

Firewall and SELinux Considerations

Cockpit listens on **port 9090**, which may be blocked by default on systems with active firewalls. To allow external access, open Cockpit's port permanently:

```
$ sudo firewall-cmd --add-service=cockpit –permanent
$ sudo firewall-cmd –reload
```

Also, ensure that **SELinux** is in **permissive** or **properly configured enforcing** mode to allow Cockpit to manage system operations. Misconfigured SELinux policies can silently block web interface features, including package actions.

When to Use Cockpit's PackageKit Plugin

Cockpit is ideal for

- **System administrators managing multiple servers**
- **Headless environments** where GUI tools aren't available
- **Remote software updates** without SSH or command-line usage
- **Monitoring server status** while applying updates in real time

However, it is **not** meant to replace full-featured GUI package managers like GNOME Software or Synaptic on desktop systems. Its strength lies in **remote management**, not user-level software discovery or graphical browsing.

NixUI/Guix Web Interfaces (NixOS, GNU Guix System)

NixUI and **Guix Web** are community-driven, experimental graphical interfaces designed to make the **declarative package management models** of Nix and Guix more accessible. These tools aim to provide a user-friendly way to manage system configurations, packages, and rollbacks—all without editing configuration files manually.

While still evolving, they are especially useful for **new users**, **desktop users**, or **system administrators** exploring Nix or Guix for the first time.

Key Features

- Browse and search installed packages, generations, and profiles.
- Roll back to previous system states (generations).
- Modify and apply declarative configurations through a graphical interface.
- Switch system or user profiles without the CLI.
- In some cases, preview system changes before applying them.

Installation Instructions

NixUI (for NixOS or Nix on Other Distros)

NixUI is available via the **Nix package manager** and works with Flakes-based configurations. To install and run it, enable Flakes (if not already enabled):

```
echo 'experimental-features = nix-command flakes' | sudo tee -a /etc/nix/nix.conf
```

Install and run NixUI:

```
nix run github:nix-gui/nix-gui
```

Alternatively, you can install it into your user environment:

```
nix profile install github:nix-gui/nix-gui
```

Then launch with

```
nix-gui
```

Note nix-gui (also known as NixUI) is still under active development. Some functionality may be incomplete or not reflect full system configuration, especially on multi-user systems.

Guix Web Interface (guix-web)

Guix does not yet have an official GUI, but **experimental web interfaces** exist (e.g., guix-web, guix-desktop). The most accessible way to try a basic interface is through **guix-web**, a community-developed project.

To install:

```
guix install guix-web
```

To run the server (usually on port 5000):

```
guix-web serve
```

Then open your browser:

```
http://localhost:5000
```

Warning Many Guix web interfaces are **minimal or read-only**. They often allow you to **view** installed packages, generations, and profiles, but **modifying configurations still requires CLI or manual edits** to config.scm.

Security and Auditing

- Always run regular security updates.
- Use apt list --upgradable, dnf check-update, and pacman -Qu to audit manually.
- Use tools like OpenSCAP, AIDE, or Lynis for deeper audit.
- Avoid installing untrusted PPAs or repos.
- Use gpg to verify source integrity when building from upstream.

Clarifying Edge Cases in Package Management

Modern Linux distributions often support multiple packaging systems simultaneously, such as APT, Snap, Flatpak, DNF, and RPM. While this offers users a wide range of flexibility, it can also lead to confusion and subtle issues. Below are common edge cases and how to handle them effectively.

Conflicts Between Snap, Flatpak, and Native Packages (APT/DNF/RPM)

It's possible to install the same application via multiple systems, like APT and Snap or DNF and Flatpak. While these can technically coexist, they often cause confusion:

- Binary conflicts: One version may override the other in your system's $PATH.

- Duplicate desktop entries: You might see two entries for the same app in your application launcher.

- Different behavior: One version may behave differently or be sandboxed.

Example

```
$ sudo apt install firefox
$ sudo snap install firefox
```

Simply use the which command to determine which version your system is running:

```
$ which firefox
/snap/bin/firefox
```

To avoid confusion, it's best to install each application using only one package source.

Flatpak Permissions and Sandboxing Limitations

Flatpak apps are designed to run in **sandboxed environments**, meaning they operate in isolation from the rest of the system. This sandboxing enhances security by limiting what apps can access by default, but it can also cause confusion when apps can't open files, interact with external devices, or communicate with other services.

Common Limitations

Out of the box, Flatpak applications

- **Cannot access external drives**, mounted volumes, or arbitrary system paths
- **May be unable to open files** from locations like /etc, /mnt, or custom folders outside the user home
- **Have restricted access to other apps and services**, which can break expected desktop integration (e.g., file pickers or shared system settings)

Managing Flatpak Permissions

You can safely customize Flatpak permissions using the following.

Flatseal (GUI Tool)

Flatseal is a user-friendly graphical application that allows you to manage Flatpak permissions on a per-app basis.

To install Flatseal:

```
flatpak install flathub com.github.tchx84.Flatseal
```

After launching it:

- Select an app from the sidebar.
- Toggle filesystem, device, network, or portal permissions as needed.
- Changes apply immediately—no restart required (See Figure 5-2).

Best for: Desktop users who prefer a visual, safe way to tweak Flatpak behavior

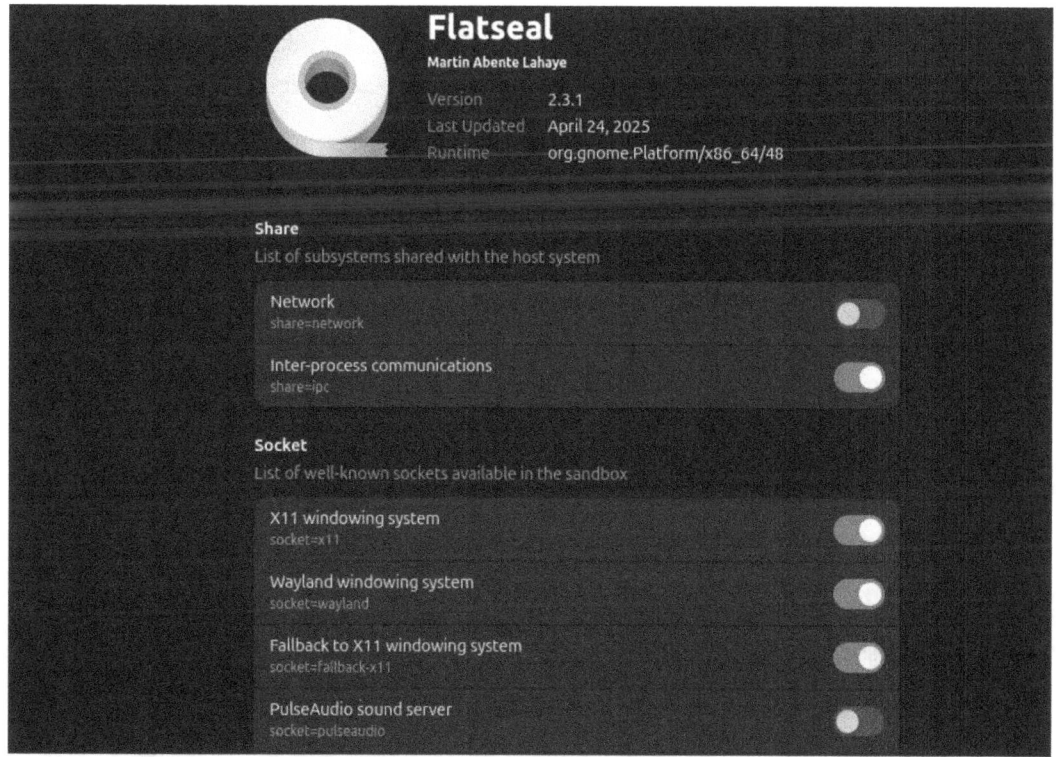

Figure 5-2. Customize Flatpak permissions using Flatseal

Terminal (Manual Overrides)

You can also grant or restrict permissions directly using the flatpak override command.
Example:

flatpak override org.mozilla.firefox --filesystem=home

This gives Firefox Flatpak access to your entire home directory.

Warning --filesystem=home significantly broadens the app's access, reducing the isolation that Flatpak provides. Use this only when absolutely necessary.

Safer, Granular Alternatives

To limit exposure, you can grant **read-only or directory-specific access**:
   Read-only access to Firefox's config folder:

```
flatpak override org.mozilla.firefox --filesystem=~/.mozilla:ro
```

   Read/write access to a specific Downloads folder:

```
flatpak override org.mozilla.firefox --filesystem=~/Downloads
```

   You can combine multiple overrides as needed to fine-tune access.

Good Practices

- **Use Flatseal** for easy management and to avoid syntax mistakes.
- **Avoid granting full home directory access** unless absolutely necessary.
- **Prefer read-only (:ro) mounts** when the app doesn't need write access.
- **Revert changes** easily with

    ```
    flatpak override --reset org.mozilla.firefox
    ```

Managing Dual Systems (e.g., Flatpak + RPM on Fedora)

On systems like Fedora, both **Flatpak** and **RPM** apps may appear side by side in GNOME Software. This can cause

- Duplicate apps (e.g., two versions of Firefox or LibreOffice)
- Wasted disk space (Flatpak bundles its own runtimes)
- Confusion over which version is running or updated

Best practice:

- Stick to **one format per app**. Use **Flatpak** for sandboxed GUI apps and **RPM** for CLI tools or apps needing full system access. Avoid installing both versions unless required.

Conclusion

Mastering package management allows us to maintain secure, efficient, and up-to-date systems. Whether you're managing a single workstation or a fleet of servers, the skills covered here are foundational to becoming a reliable Linux SysAdmin.

In the next chapter, we'll dive into shell scripting, one of the most powerful tools in a system administrator's toolkit. We'll explore how to automate repetitive tasks, create custom scripts, and use scheduling tools like cron.

CHAPTER 6

Introduction to Shell Scripting

Shell scripting is at the heart of Linux system administration. It's a powerful way to automate tasks, configure systems, manage users, and orchestrate system services. Whether you're writing a simple script to clean up logs or a complex one to deploy software across multiple servers, mastering shell scripting is essential.

In this chapter, we will start from the basics and progressively build toward more advanced scripting techniques, all tailored for new Linux system administrators. The following is an overview of what we're going to cover in this chapter:

1. What Is Shell Scripting?
2. Why Shell Scripting Matters in Linux System Administration
3. Understanding the Shell
   - Bash and Other Shells
   - The Shell as a Command Interpreter
4. Shell Scripting Basics
   - Creating Your First Shell Script
   - File Permissions and the Shebang (#!)
   - Running Scripts
5. Variables
   - Declaring Variables
   - Environment Variables
   - Quoting: Single vs. Double

CHAPTER 6 INTRODUCTION TO SHELL SCRIPTING

6. User Input and Output
   - read Command
   - Echo and Print
   - Command Substitution
7. Conditional Statements
   - if, else, and elif
   - test and [ ] Conditions
   - Case Statements
8. Loops
   - for Loops
   - while Loops
   - until Loops
9. Functions in Shell Scripts
   - Defining and Calling Functions
   - Function Scope and Returning Values
10. Error Handling and Debugging with set
    - Exit Status ($?)
    - set -x and set -e
    - Logging Errors
11. Automating Tasks with Shell Scripts
    - Backups
    - Monitoring and alerts
    - Log rotation
12. Scheduling Scripts with cron
13. Best Practices in shell scripting

What Is Shell Scripting?

Shell scripting refers to writing a sequence of commands for the shell to execute. These scripts are text files containing commands just as you would type them in the command line. However, when written in a script, these commands can be automated, repeated, modified, and scheduled.

A shell script is essentially a program written for the shell. Most Linux systems use **Bash** (Bourne Again SHell), but there are other shells such as **sh**, **zsh**, **ksh**, and **csh**.

Why Shell Scripting Matters in Linux System Administration

As a system administrator, many tasks are repetitive, creating users, updating packages, backing up data, and monitoring disk space. Instead of doing these manually each time, a script can perform them for you, saving time and reducing human error.

Shell scripting can

- Automate routine administrative tasks.
- Perform batch processing.
- Generate reports.
- Monitor system health.
- Deploy configurations.
- Chain together complex commands.

Whether you're managing one machine or hundreds, **shell scripting transforms repetitive work into efficient, error-resistant processes**. For Linux system administrators, it's not just a handy tool—**it's an essential skill**.

CHAPTER 6   INTRODUCTION TO SHELL SCRIPTING

Understanding the Shell

Bash and Other Shells

The shell is the command-line interpreter that provides a user interface for Unix and Linux systems. Bash is the most used shell in Linux distributions. Others include

- sh: The original Bourne Shell
- ksh: KornShell
- zsh: Z Shell
- csh: C Shell

While this chapter focuses on Bash, the concepts are broadly applicable across other shells.

The Shell as a Command Interpreter

The shell interprets user input (commands) and interacts with the kernel to execute them. When you write a script, you're essentially automating a series of these commands.

Shell Scripting Basics

Creating Your First Shell Script

Let's write a basic script:

```
#!/bin/bash
echo "Hello, world!"
```

Save this as hello.sh.

File Permissions and the Shebang (#!)

- #!/bin/bash tells the system to use Bash to run the script. This line must be the first in the file.

To make the script executable:

```
$ chmod +x hello.sh
```

Running Scripts

You can run the script in a few ways:

```
$ ./hello.sh
$ bash hello.sh
$ sh hello.sh
```

Using ./hello.sh requires execution permissions and ensures the shebang line is respected.

Variables

Variables in shell scripts are used to store and manipulate data such as strings, numbers, file paths, or command results. Unlike statically typed languages, shell variables do not require a data type declaration; everything is treated as a string by default.

Declaring Variables

```
$ name="Alice"
$ echo "Hello, $name"
Hello, Alice
```

Note No spaces around the equals sign. Variables are case-sensitive.

Environment Variables

Environment variables are predefined variables provided by the system, like $USER, $HOME, and $PATH. They are available to all programs running in your shell.

```
$ echo "Your home directory is $HOME"
```

Your home directory is /home/alice.

To create your own environment variable that child processes can inherit:

```
$ export VAR=value
```

Quoting: Single vs. Double

Quotes control how strings and variables are interpreted.

- **Double quotes** allow variable and command substitution.
- **Single quotes** treat the content literally (no expansion).

Example:

```
echo "User is $USER"
echo 'User is $USER'
User is alice
User is $USER
```

User Input and Output

Interacting with users makes scripts dynamic. You can prompt for data using read and display messages using echo or printf.

To read user input:

```
$ echo "Enter your name:"
$ read username
$ echo "Hello, $username"
Enter your name:
Bob
Hello, Bob
```

Echo and Print

echo is simple, while printf gives you more control over formatting:

```
$ echo "Simple message"
$ printf "Formatted: %s\n" "$username"
Simple message
Formatted: Bob
```

Command Substitution

You can capture the output of a command into a variable using $(...):

```
$ today=$(date)
$ echo "Today's date is $today"
Today's date is Tue Aug  5 14:00:00 UTC 2025
```

Conditional Statements

Conditions help your script make decisions based on logic, like checking if a file exists or comparing values.

if, else, and elif

```
if [ "$age" -ge 18 ]; then
    echo "You are an adult."
elif [ "$age" -lt 18 ]; then
    echo "You are a minor."
else
    echo "Invalid age."
Fi
You are an adult.
```

test and [ ] Conditions

Both work the same. Use them to compare strings, numbers, and check files:

```
if test "$var" = "value"
if [ "$var" = "value" ]
```

Common tests:

- -f FILE: True if file exists and is a regular file
- -d DIR: True if directory exists
- -z STR: True if string is empty
- -n STR: True if string is not empty

Case Statements

Great for matching multiple values without using lots of if/elif.

```
case $1 in
    start)
        echo "Starting..."
        ;;
    stop)
        echo "Stopping..."
        ;;
    *)
        echo "Usage: $0 {start|stop}"
        ;;
esac
```

Loops

Loops allow you to repeat commands until a condition is met or over a range of items.

for Loops

```
for i in 1 2 3; do
    echo "Number $i"
done
Number 1
Number 2
Number 3
```

while Loops

Loops until a condition becomes false:

```
count=1
while [ $count -le 5 ]; do
    echo "Count is $count"
    ((count++))
done

Count is 1
Count is 2
Count is 3
```

until Loops

Runs until the condition becomes true:

```
until [ "$response" = "yes" ]; do
    echo "Do you agree? (yes/no)"
    read response
done
```

CHAPTER 6   INTRODUCTION TO SHELL SCRIPTING

Functions in Shell Scripts

Functions help you organize your code into reusable blocks, like mini-scripts inside scripts:

```
greet() {
    echo "Hello, $1"
}
greet Alice

Hello, Alice
```

Returning Values

You can capture the output or return an integer:

```
get_date() {
    date
}
today=$(get_date)
echo "$today"

Tue Aug  5 14:00:00 UTC 2025
```

Error Handling and Debugging

Exit Status

Every command returns an exit status:

- 0 = success
- Non-zero = error

```
ls /tmp
echo "Exit status: $?"
```

Debugging with set

set -x: Debug mode, shows commands as they execute.
  set -e: Exit immediately on error.
  Useful during script testing.

Logging Errors

Redirect output:

```
$ command 2> error.log
```

Automating Tasks with Shell Scripts

Shell scripts are perfect for automating system administration tasks such as backups, monitoring, log rotation, user management, patch deployment, or reporting. Below are some developed and practical automation examples you can study, adapt, and deploy in real-world scenarios.

Automated Full System Backup with Logging and Compression

Objective

In this example, we'll automate a full system backup (excluding sensitive or unnecessary directories like /proc, /sys, /tmp, etc.), compress it, and keep a log of all operations. The script will also remove backups older than seven days to save space.

Note This script performs a full filesystem data backup excluding system and runtime directories. It is not a bare-metal recovery solution. For full system recovery including OS reinstallation, tools like Clonezilla or dd, which create disk images, are recommended.

Create the script file:

```
$ sudo nano /usr/local/bin/full_backup.sh
#!/bin/bash
=== CONFIGURATION ===
BACKUP_SRC="/" BACKUP_DEST="/backups" LOG_FILE="/var/log/system_backup.log"
EXCLUDE_FILE="/etc/backup_exclude.txt" RETENTION_DAYS=7 DATE=$(date +%F_%H-%M) BACKUP_FILE="$BACKUP_DEST/full_backup_$DATE.tar.gz"
=== CREATE EXCLUDE FILE IF IT DOES NOT EXIST ===
if [ ! -f "$EXCLUDE_FILE" ]; then cat << EOF > "$EXCLUDE_FILE" /proc /sys /tmp /dev /run /mnt /media /lost+found EOF chmod 644 "$EXCLUDE_FILE" fi
=== LOG START ===
echo "[$DATE] Starting system backup..." >> "$LOG_FILE"
=== CREATE BACKUP DIRECTORY ===
mkdir -p "$BACKUP_DEST" if [ $? -ne 0 ]; then echo "[$DATE] ERROR: Could not create backup destination directory: $BACKUP_DEST" >> "$LOG_FILE" exit 1 fi
=== CREATE BACKUP ===
tar -czpf "$BACKUP_FILE" --exclude-from="$EXCLUDE_FILE" "$BACKUP_SRC" >> "$LOG_FILE" 2>&1 if [ $? -eq 0 ]; then echo "[$DATE] Backup completed successfully: $BACKUP_FILE" >> "$LOG_FILE" else echo "[$DATE] ERROR: Backup failed." >> "$LOG_FILE" exit 1 fi
=== DELETE OLD BACKUPS WITH ERROR CHECKING ===
if find "$BACKUP_DEST" -name "*.tar.gz" -type f -mtime +$RETENTION_DAYS -exec rm -f {} \; >> "$LOG_FILE" 2>&1; then echo "[$DATE] Old backups cleaned." >> "$LOG_FILE" else echo "[$DATE] WARNING: Could not clean old backups." >> "$LOG_FILE" fi
=== LOG COMPLETION ===
echo "[$DATE] Backup process finished." >> "$LOG_FILE"
```

Explanation:

- Uses tar with compression to create timestamped backup archives
- Logs all operations, including errors and cleanup activities, to /var/log/system_backup.log
- Creates the exclude file only if it doesn't already exist, preserving any custom directory exclusions added by the administrator

- Automatically removes backups older than seven days, with error checking and logging to alert if cleanup fails
- Clearly clarifies that this is a full filesystem data backup—not a bare-metal recovery solution

Make it executable:

```
$ sudo chmod +x /usr/local/bin/full_backup.sh
```

Run manually:

```
$ sudo /usr/local/bin/full_backup.sh
```

Automated Security Patch Installation with Reporting

Objective

In this example, we'll automatically install available security updates daily, log actions, and email a summary to the administrator.

> **Important note** This script is designed for **Debian/Ubuntu-based systems** using apt for package management. It will **not work** on non-Debian distributions like Red Hat, CentOS, Fedora, or Arch Linux, which use different package managers (dnf, yum, or pacman). For those systems, you should use their respective commands to manage security updates, such as
> - CentOS/RHEL: sudo dnf update --security -y
> - Fedora: sudo dnf update --security -y
> - Arch Linux: sudo pacman -Syu

Create the script file:

```
$ sudo nano /usr/local/bin/security_update.sh
```

Paste the script:

```bash
#!/bin/bash
=== CONFIGURATION ===
LOG_FILE="/var/log/security_updates.log" DATE=$(date "+%F %T")
EMAIL="admin@linux.com" HOSTNAME=$(hostname)
=== LOG START ===
echo "[$DATE] Starting security update check..." >> "$LOG_FILE"
=== UPDATE SYSTEM ===
apt-get update >> "$LOG_FILE" 2>&1 apt-get upgrade -y >> "$LOG_FILE" 2>&1
=== CHECK EXIT STATUS ===
if [ $? -eq 0 ]; then echo "[$DATE] Security updates installed successfully on $HOSTNAME." >> "$LOG_FILE" else echo "[$DATE] ERROR: Failed to install security updates." >> "$LOG_FILE" fi
=== SEND REPORT ===
mail -s "[$HOSTNAME] Daily Security Update Report" "$EMAIL" < "$LOG_FILE"
```

Explanation:

- Automatically updates the package list and applies available security updates
- Logs all update steps and any errors to /var/log/security_updates.log
- Sends a daily email report with the log contents to the administrator
- Filters security-related packages in the log for easier review
- Designed specifically for Debian/Ubuntu systems using apt

Make it executable:

```
$ sudo chmod +x /usr/local/bin/security_update.sh
```

Run manually:

```
$ sudo /usr/local/bin/security_update.sh
```

Server Resource Monitoring and Alert System

Objective

Monitor CPU, memory, and disk usage. If usage crosses threshold limits, send alerts via email.

Create the script:

```
$ sudo nano /usr/local/bin/resource_monitor.sh
#!/bin/bash
=== CONFIGURATION ===
CPU_THRESHOLD=80 MEM_THRESHOLD=90 DISK_THRESHOLD=90 EMAIL="admin@linux.com" HOSTNAME=$(hostname) ALERT_LOG="/var/log/sys_alert.log" DATE=$(date "+%F %T")
=== GATHER METRICS ===
CPU usage: 'top' command output can vary between systems.
This extracts the idle CPU percentage and subtracts it from 100.
Note: This method can be fragile across different Linux distributions.
cpu=$(top -bn1 | grep "Cpu(s)" | awk '{print 100 - $8}')
Memory usage: percentage of used memory
mem=$(free | awk '/Mem/ {printf("%.0f", $3/$2 * 100)}')
Disk usage: percentage used on root partition
disk=$(df / | awk 'NR==2 {print $5}' | sed 's/%//')
alert=""
=== THRESHOLD CHECKS ===
Integer comparison is done by stripping decimal part (${cpu%.*})
This ensures safe numeric comparison in bash.
if (( ${cpu%.*} > CPU_THRESHOLD )); then alert+="High CPU usage: $cpu%\n" fi
if (( mem > MEM_THRESHOLD )); then alert+="High Memory usage: $mem%\n" fi
if (( disk > DISK_THRESHOLD )); then alert+="High Disk usage: $disk%\n" fi
=== SEND ALERT IF ANY THRESHOLD EXCEEDED ===
if [ -n "$alert" ]; then echo -e "[$DATE] Alert on $HOSTNAME:\n$alert" >> "$ALERT_LOG" echo -e "$alert" | mail -s "[$HOSTNAME] System Resource Alert" "$EMAIL" else echo "[$DATE] System health normal." >> "$ALERT_LOG" fi
```

Explanation:

- Threshold-based alerting: Checks CPU, memory, and disk usage against configured limits

- Multiple metrics combined: Aggregates all alerts into a single notification

- Conditional alerts: Sends email only if usage crosses thresholds

- Comprehensive logging: Records both normal and alert events for auditing

- Integer comparisons: Uses parameter expansion ${cpu%.*} to safely convert CPU usage to integer for comparison

Note on CPU measurement The method using top can be brittle depending on the Linux version. For greater reliability, tools like mpstat (from the sysstat package) are recommended for production environments.

Make it executable:

```
$ sudo chmod +x /usr/local/bin/resource_monitor.sh
```

Run manually:

```
$ sudo /usr/local/bin/resource_monitor.sh
```

Automated Log Analyzer and Report Generator

Objective

Parse log files (/var/log/auth.log), extract login attempts (both successful and failed), generate daily reports, and email them.

Create the script:

```
$ sudo nano /usr/local/bin/log_report.sh
```

Paste the following script:

```bash
#!/bin/bash
=== CONFIGURATION ===
Note: This script is for Debian-based systems using /var/log/auth.log.
For RHEL-based systems, change LOG_FILE to /var/log/secure.
if [[ -f /var/log/auth.log ]]; then LOG_FILE="/var/log/auth.log" elif [[ -f /var/log/secure ]]; then LOG_FILE="/var/log/secure" else echo "Error: No supported authentication log file found." exit 1 fi
REPORT_FILE="/tmp/login_report_$(date +%F).txt" EMAIL="admin@linux.com"
=== GENERATE REPORT ===
echo "Login Report for $(date +%F)" > "$REPORT_FILE" echo "===============================" >> "$REPORT_FILE"
echo -e "\nFailed Login Attempts:" >> "$REPORT_FILE" grep "Failed password" "$LOG_FILE" | awk '{print $1, $2, $3, $(NF-3), $(NF)}' >> "$REPORT_FILE"
echo -e "\nSuccessful Logins:" >> "$REPORT_FILE" grep "Accepted password" "$LOG_FILE" | awk '{print $1, $2, $3, $(NF-3), $(NF)}' >> "$REPORT_FILE"
echo -e "\nTop 5 IPs with Failed Logins:" >> "$REPORT_FILE" grep "Failed password" "$LOG_FILE" | awk '{print $(NF)}' | sort | uniq -c | sort -nr | head -5 >> "$REPORT_FILE"
=== SEND REPORT ===
mail -s "Daily SSH Login Report" "$EMAIL" < "$REPORT_FILE"
```

Explanation:

- Generates a daily summary of login activity (both failed and successful)

- Helps detect brute-force attacks by highlighting failed attempts and the top offending IP addresses

- Easy to modify for other authentication methods or log systems (e.g., SSH key logins, journalctl)

- Sends concise, scannable reports via email to keep administrators informed

CHAPTER 6 INTRODUCTION TO SHELL SCRIPTING

Make it executable:

```
$ sudo chmod +x /usr/local/bin/log_report.sh
```

Run manually:

```
$ sudo /usr/local/bin/log_report.sh
```

Automated User Account Creation and Configuration
Objective

Create multiple users from a CSV file, assign them default passwords, create their home directories, and force them to change their password on first login.

Prepare the CSV file:

```
$ sudo nano users.csv
```

Paste:

```
username,fullname
jdoe,John Doe
asmith,Alice Smith
```

Create the script:

```
$ sudo nano create_users.sh
```

Paste the script below:

```bash
#!/bin/bash

# === CONFIGURATION ===
USER_FILE="users.csv"
DEFAULT_PASS="Linux@2025"

# === PROCESS USERS ===
while IFS=, read -r username fullname; do
    if id "$username" &>/dev/null; then
        echo "User $username already exists. Skipping..."
```

```
    else
        useradd -m -c "$fullname" "$username"
        echo "$username:$DEFAULT_PASS" | chpasswd
        passwd -e "$username"
        echo "User $username ($fullname) created."
    fi
done < <(tail -n +2 "$USER_FILE")
```

Explanation:

- Reads user data from a structured CSV file (skipping the header).
- Automatically sets default passwords (Linux@2025) for each user.
- Expires passwords immediately to force users to change them on first login.
- Checks if the user already exists to avoid duplication.
- The line done < <(tail -n +2 "$USER_FILE") uses **process substitution**, which treats the output of tail as a readable file input. This is a clean and efficient way to skip the CSV header while reading the rest of the lines.

Make the script executable and run it:

```
$ sudo chmod +x create_users.sh
$ sudo ./create_users.sh
```

```
$sudo ./create_users.sh
useradd: invalid user name '': use --badname to ignore
chpasswd: (user ) pam_chauthtok() failed, error:
Authentication token manipulation error
chpasswd: (line 1, user ) password not changed
passwd: user '' does not exist
User () created.
passwd: password changed.
User jdoe (John Doe ) created.
useradd: invalid user name '': use --badname to ignore
chpasswd: (user ) pam_chauthtok() failed, error:
Authentication token manipulation error
chpasswd: (line 1, user ) password not changed
passwd: user '' does not exist
User () created.
passwd: password changed.
User asmith (Alice Smith ) created.
$
```

Scheduling Scripts with cron

One of the greatest advantages of shell scripting is automation, and that power is magnified by combining scripts with the cron scheduling service.

cron is a time-based job scheduler in Unix-like operating systems. It enables system administrators and users to schedule scripts and commands to run

- At fixed times (e.g., 2 AM every day)
- On specific days of the week
- Every few minutes or hours
- On system reboot or shutdown

This means you can automate backups, updates, cleanups, reporting, and monitoring, all without lifting a finger once it's set up.

How cron Works

cron uses a special configuration file called the crontab (cron table), where you define what command to run and when to run it. Each user has their own crontab file, and there's also a system-wide one located at /etc/crontab.

How It Works Internally

1. The cron daemon (crond) runs in the background.
2. Every minute, it checks all crontabs for jobs that should be run at that time.
3. If a job's schedule matches the current time, cron executes the associated command/script.

Editing Your Crontab

To edit your personal crontab:

```
$ crontab -e
```

The first time you run this, it may prompt you to choose an editor (nano, vim, etc.). After that, you'll see a blank or pre-filled crontab file.

Each line in a crontab represents a scheduled job with this structure:

```
* * * * * /path/to/command
| | | | |
| | | | +----- Day of the week (0 - 7) (Sunday = 0 or 7)
| | | +------- Month (1 - 12)
| | +--------- Day of the month (1 - 31)
| +----------- Hour (0 - 23)
+------------- Minute (0 - 59)
```

Common Examples of cron Jobs

Run a backup every day at 2 AM:

```
0 2 * * * /usr/local/bin/backup.sh
```

Run a temp cleanup every hour:

```
0 * * * * /usr/local/bin/clean_tmp.sh
```

Run a log monitoring script every 15 minutes:

```
*/15 * * * * /usr/local/bin/check_logs.sh
```

Run a report generator at 6 PM on weekdays (Mon-Fri):

```
0 18 * * 1-5 /usr/local/bin/report.sh
```

Run a system info script every Monday at 8 AM:

```
0 8 * * 1 /usr/local/bin/sysinfo.sh
```

Advanced Scheduling Patterns

Multiple Values

Run every day at 3 AM and 6 AM:

```
0 3,6 * * * /usr/local/bin/dual_run.sh
```

Interval Runs

Run every 5 minutes:

```
*/5 * * * * /usr/local/bin/every_5_min.sh
```

Run only on the first of every month:

```
0 0 1 * * /usr/local/bin/monthly_maintenance.sh
```

Run the Script at Reboot

To run a script every time the system reboots:

```
@reboot /usr/local/bin/startup_tasks.sh
```

This is useful for things like

- Restoring a network mount
- Starting a local web service
- Sending system health alerts

Permissions and Environment in cron

cron runs in a minimal shell environment, it doesn't load your full ~/.bashrc or ~/.profile. So variables like PATH, HOME, or custom exports might not be set, causing scripts to fail if they rely on them.

Solutions

1. Always use absolute paths in scripts (e.g., /usr/bin/tar, /usr/bin/python3).

2. Add environment variables explicitly in your crontab:

   PATH=/usr/local/sbin:/usr/local/bin:/usr/sbin:/usr/bin:/sbin:/bin

3. Export variables inside your script if needed.

Logging and Output

By default, cron doesn't send output to your terminal. Instead:

- Standard output and errors can be mailed to the user.
- Or they can be redirected to log files.

Example with Logging

0 3 * * * /usr/local/bin/db_backup.sh >> /var/log/db_backup.log 2>&1

- >> appends output to the log file.
- 2>&1 sends both stdout and stderr to the same log.

To disable email notifications, you can redirect output to /dev/null:

```
0 3 * * * /usr/local/bin/db_backup.sh > /dev/null 2>&1
```

Viewing Crontab Entries

```
$ crontab -l
```

Remove Your Crontab

```
$ crontab -r
```

Be careful, there's no confirmation prompt for "**-r**".

Edit the System-Wide Crontab

```
$ sudo nano /etc/crontab
```

Format of this file is slightly different, it includes a user field:

```
0 1 * * * root /usr/local/bin/sys_backup.sh
```

Viewing cron Job Logs

Traditional syslog (Some Distributions)

```
$ cat /var/log/cron
```

Using journalctl (on systemd-Based Systems)

```
$ journalctl -u cron
```

Or grep for cron-related entries:

```
$ journalctl | grep CRON
```

You can also check logs from your script itself, if you're writing output to a file, for example, /var/log/mytask.log.

Testing Your cron Jobs

Before relying on cron, always

1. Test the script manually to confirm it works.

2. Run the script with its full path.

3. Check file permissions—the user running cron must have permission to execute the script.

4. Watch for dependency issues—if the script calls other programs or needs environment variables, define them explicitly.

cron Troubleshooting Tips

- Script not running? Add echo statements and redirect output to a log file.

- Use which to get the full path to commands:

    ```
    $ which tar
    $ which python3
    ```

- Use bash -x script.sh for debugging your script.

- Add set -e and set -x at the top of your script for early exit and debug tracing.

Real-World Use Case: Scheduled Backup with cron

Let's tie everything together with an actual deployment.

Task

We want to back up /etc and /var/www every night at 1 AM, log the activity, and retain backups for seven days:

```
Script: /usr/local/bin/nightly_backup.sh
#!/bin/bash
 set -e # Exit immediately on error
```

```
=== CONFIGURATION ===
BACKUP_DIR="/backups" DATE=$(date +%F_%H-%M) LOG_FILE="/var/log/nightly_backup.log"
=== ENSURE BACKUP DIRECTORY EXISTS ===
mkdir -p "$BACKUP_DIR"
=== CREATE BACKUPS ===
tar -czf "$BACKUP_DIR/etc_backup_$DATE.tar.gz" /etc >> "$LOG_FILE" 2>&1
tar -czf "$BACKUP_DIR/www_backup_$DATE.tar.gz" /var/www >> "$LOG_FILE" 2>&1
=== CLEAN UP OLD BACKUPS ===
find "$BACKUP_DIR" -name "*backup*.tar.gz" -type f -mtime +7 -delete >> "$LOG_FILE" 2>&1
=== LOG COMPLETION ===
echo "[$DATE] Nightly backup completed successfully." >> "$LOG_FILE"
```

Make the script executable:

```
sudo chmod +x /usr/local/bin/nightly_backup.sh
```

Run the script manually to test:

```
sudo /usr/local/bin/nightly_backup.sh
```

Set Up the Cron Job

To schedule the backup to run nightly at 1 AM, add the following to your crontab:

```
0 1 * * * /usr/local/bin/nightly_backup.sh
```

Use crontab -e to edit your user's crontab or place it in /etc/crontab or a cron.d file for system-wide use. For more information on cron scheduling, visit the Ubuntu CronHowTo.

Explanation:

- Uses tar to compress and archive both /etc and /var/www.
- Filenames include both date and time (e.g., etc_backup_2025-09-30_01-00.tar.gz) to prevent accidental overwriting.
- Automatically removes backup files older than seven days, but only those matching the backup filename pattern (*_backup_*.tar.gz).

- Logs all output and errors to /var/log/nightly_backup.log for auditing.
- Uses set -e to ensure the script exits on any failure, preventing false success logs.
- Designed to be safely and silently run via cron in unattended mode.

Best Practices

Follow these to write clean, secure, and reliable scripts:

- **Shebang used**: #!/bin/bash
- **Quoted variables** to prevent globbing or word-splitting
- **Error handling** with set -e
- **Clear filenaming** with timestamps
- **Scoped file deletion** to prevent collateral data loss
- **Centralized logging** for troubleshooting
- **Modular and readable** script with clearly separated logic blocks

Conclusion

Shell scripting is an indispensable tool for any Linux system administrator. It empowers you to automate complex tasks, enforce consistency, and work more efficiently. This chapter has introduced you to the fundamentals: from writing your first script to using loops, conditionals, and scheduling tasks with cron. Mastering shell scripting will elevate your sysadmin skills and give you the power to control and automate nearly every aspect of a Linux environment.

In the next chapter, we'll shift our focus to system monitoring and performance. We'll explore tools like top, htop, and journalctl for monitoring processes and logs, learn how to identify performance bottlenecks, and discover techniques for tuning system parameters.

CHAPTER 7

System Monitoring and Performance

Managing a Linux system isn't just about installing software and making things run; it's also about keeping everything running smoothly. This is where system monitoring and performance tuning come into play.

In this chapter, we'll walk through essential tools and techniques to help you understand how your Linux system is performing, how to interpret various statistics, and what to do when things aren't working as efficiently as they should. You don't need to be a Linux guru to get started; you just need a solid foundation, and that's what we'll build here.

Tools for Monitoring System Performance

One of the strengths of Linux is the wealth of tools available to monitor system performance. These tools help you understand how much CPU, memory, and disk your applications and services are using in real time.

top, htop, and Other Monitoring Tools

top

top is a built-in command-line tool available on almost all Linux distributions. It provides a real-time, dynamic view of system processes, sorted by CPU usage by default. To launch top, just open your terminal and type

```
$ top
top - 12:05:40 up 5 days,  2:10,  1 user,  load average: 0.47, 0.52, 0.58
Tasks: 215 total,   2 running, 213 sleeping,   0 stopped,   0 zombie
%Cpu(s):  3.2 us,  1.0 sy,  0.0 ni, 95.4 id,  0.3 wa,  0.0 hi,  0.1 si,  0.0 st
```

Explanation of %Cpu(s) fields:

- us – User processes (non-kernel tasks)
- sy – System processes (kernel tasks)
- ni – Processes running with adjusted "nice" values
- id – Idle CPU time
- wa – Time spent waiting on I/O
- hi – Hardware interrupts
- si – Software interrupts
- st – Stolen time (CPU time taken by hypervisor in VMs)

Tip Use the P key inside top to sort by CPU usage or M to sort by memory usage.

htop

htop is an enhanced alternative to top. It provides a more readable, colorful, and interactive user interface. You can scroll through the list of processes, kill tasks, and sort using function keys.

Installation

Debian/Ubuntu

```
$ sudo apt install htop
```

RHEL/CentOS/Fedora

```
$ sudo dnf install htop
To use:
$ htop
```

Why choose htop over top?

- Better visual layout
- Easier navigation
- Mouse support

vmstat: Virtual Memory Statistics

vmstat reports CPU, memory, swap, IO, system, and process statistics.

Installation

vmstat is part of the procps or sysstat package depending on the distribution.

Debian/Ubuntu

```
$ sudo apt update
$ sudo apt install procps
```

RHEL/CentOS/Fedora

```
$ sudo dnf install procps-ng
```

Usage

```
$ vmstat 2 5

procs -----------memory---------- ---swap-- -----io---- -system-- ------cpu-----
 r  b   swpd   free   buff  cache   si   so    bi    bo   in   cs us sy id wa st
 2  0      0 500000  12000 340000    0    0     2     1  100  200 20 10 70  0  0
```

Explanation:

- 2: Update interval in seconds
- 5: Number of updates
- r: Number of processes waiting for CPU
- free: Free memory

- si/so: Swap in/out

- us, sy, id, wa: CPU usage—user, system, idle, wait

> **Note** High wa (IO wait) means your system is likely waiting on slow disk access.

Optional Enhancements

Add pidstat for Per-Process Statistics

pidstat (from the **sysstat** package) provides per-process CPU, memory, and I/O statistics over time—very useful for troubleshooting.

Example:

```
$ pidstat 2 5
```

Table 7-1 provides common system performance symptoms, the recommended tools to diagnose them, example commands, and key indicators to look for in the output.

Table 7-1. Troubleshooting Table

Symptom	Tool	Command	What to Look For
High CPU usage	vmstat	vmstat 2 5	High us or sy values
Memory leaks	vmstat	vmstat 2 5	Low free memory, high swpd
I/O bottlenecks	vmstat	vmstat 2 5	High wa and bi/bo values
Per-process CPU	pidstat	pidstat 2 5	Processes with high %CPU

iostat: Input/Output Statistics

iostat shows how busy your disks are. It's ideal for identifying disk bottlenecks.

Installation

Debian/Ubuntu

```
$ sudo apt update
$ sudo apt install sysstat
```

CHAPTER 7   SYSTEM MONITORING AND PERFORMANCE

RHEL/CentOS/Fedora

```
$ sudo dnf install sysstat
```

Note iostat works immediately after installation and does **not** require the sysstat service to be enabled for interactive use.

Enable and start the sysstat service only if you want to collect **periodic historical statistics** (e.g., for sar):

```
$ sudo systemctl enable --now sysstat
```

Usage

```
$ iostat -xz 1 5

Device:    tps     kB_read/s    kB_wrtn/s    %util
sda        2.3     1500         500          30.00
```

Explanation:

- -x: Show extended statistics (e.g., queue size, wait time, service time).
- -z: Suppress output for devices with zero activity.
- 1 5: Update every one second, five times.

Key Metrics

- tps: Transfers per second (number of I/O operations per second)
- kB_read/s: Kilobytes read per second
- kB_wrtn/s: Kilobytes written per second
- %util: Percentage of time the device was busy handling I/O operations

> **Tip** If %util is consistently above 80–90%, the disk may be a performance bottleneck.

A %util near 100% indicates the device is fully saturated and may not be able to handle additional I/O efficiently.

free: Memory Usage Snapshot

free gives a quick view of RAM and swap usage. It's often the first tool used to check memory-related issues.

Installation

Usually comes pre-installed on most Linux systems. If not, see the following.

Debian/Ubuntu

```
$ sudo apt install procps
```

RHEL/CentOS

```
$ sudo dnf install procps-ng
```

Usage

```
$ free -h
              total        used        free      shared  buff/cache   available
Mem:           7.8G        2.1G        3.0G        100M        2.7G        5.3G
Swap:          2.0G          0B        2.0G
```

Explanation:

- used: Memory currently in use
- free: Completely unused memory
- buff/cache: Temporary system use, *can be reclaimed*
- available: Real amount of memory available to apps

Note If your used memory seems high, don't panic. Linux uses free RAM for caching to speed things up. What matters more is the "available" column, which shows how much memory your applications can still use safely.

The **available** column is the most reliable indicator of application headroom—it's the number to watch when assessing if your system is running low on usable memory.

dstat: Versatile All-in-One Resource Monitor

dstat provides real-time monitoring for CPU, memory, network, disk, and more—all in a single view. It combines the functionality of tools like vmstat, iostat, netstat, and others, making it useful for quick, high-level system diagnostics.

Installation

Debian/Ubuntu

```
$ sudo apt update
$ sudo apt install dstat
```

RHEL/CentOS

```
$ sudo dnf install dstat
```

Note On some **RHEL/Fedora** systems, dstat may not be included in the base repositories. You may need to install it from **EPEL** (Extra Packages for Enterprise Linux), or consider using modern alternatives like vmstat, iostat, and pidstat.

Basic Usage

```
$ dstat

----total-cpu-usage---- -dsk/total- -net/total- ---paging-- ---system--
usr sys idl wai hiq siq| read  writ| recv  send|  in   out | int   csw
```

CHAPTER 7 SYSTEM MONITORING AND PERFORMANCE

2	1	96	0	0	0	0	0	0	0	0	0	0	1234	4567
1	0	99	0	0	0	0	0	512B	256B	0	0	0	1187	4472
3	1	96	0	0	0	0	0	1KB	1KB	0	0	0	1298	4675

Explanation:

usr	% CPU used by user space
sys	% CPU used by system (kernel)
idl	% CPU idle (not used)
wai	% CPU waiting on I/O
hiq/siq	% CPU used by hardware/software interrupts
read, writ	Total disk read/write in blocks/sec
recv, send	Network receive/send rates
in, out	Paging activity (swap in/out)
int, csw	Interrupts and context switches per second

To monitor specific components:

```
$ dstat -c --top-cpu -d -n --output perf.csv
----total-cpu-usage---- -dsk/total- -net/total- --top-cpu--
usr sys idl wai hiq siq| read writ| recv send| process
  5   2  90   1   0   0|  1k   2k |  20k  10k | firefox
```

Explanation:

- -c: CPU stats.
- --top-cpu: Show the top CPU-consuming process.
- -d: Disk stats.
- -n: Network stats.
- --output: Export data to a CSV file.

Tip Use --output to save performance data during tests or stress testing and review it later in a spreadsheet.

When to Use Which Tool

- Use free when you want a quick overview of memory.
- Use vmstat to watch overall system activity.
- Use iostat when troubleshooting disk latency or IO overload.
- Use dstat when you want a real-time dashboard that includes everything at once.

Checking Memory and Disk Usage

Understanding what resources your Linux system is using is critical for maintaining performance and stability.

Memory Usage

The free -h command gives a quick summary:

```
$ free -h
              total        used        free      shared  buff/cache   available
Mem:           7.7G        2.1G        3.0G        110M        2.6G        5.1G
Swap:          2.0G          0B        2.0G
```

Explanation:

- total: Total physical RAM
- used: Actively used by processes
- free: Completely unused memory
- buff/cache: Used for filesystem cache (Linux uses free RAM as cache to speed up disk access)
- available: RAM available for new applications without swapping

Using vmstat

Run

```
$ vmstat 2 5
```

```
procs -----------memory---------- ---swap-- -----io---- -system-- ------cpu-----
 r  b   swpd   free   buff  cache   si   so    bi    bo   in   cs us sy id wa st
 2  0      0 309284  14844 743360    0    0     0     1   59   85  5  1 93  1  0
```

Explanation:

- swpd: Swap used
- free, buff, cache: Memory statistics
- si/so: Swap in/out (non-zero values mean the system is actively swapping)
- us, sy, id: CPU usage—user, system, idle
- b: Number of processes blocked (usually waiting for I/O)

Tip A **consistently non-zero b value**, especially when combined with a **high wa (IO wait)** percentage, often indicates an I/O bottleneck—the system is waiting on slow disk or storage operations.

Disk Usage

Check disk space with

```
$ df -h
```

```
Filesystem      Size  Used Avail Use% Mounted on
/dev/sda1        50G   30G   18G  63% /
tmpfs           3.8G     0  3.8G   0% /dev/shm
```

Explanation:
Size: Total disk space

Used: Used space

Avail: Available free space

Use%: Percent usage (watch for partitions over 80%)

Using du: Disk Usage per Directory

Run

```
$ sudo du -sh /var/log
120M    /var/log
```

Use this to identify large folders taking up space.

Note Running out of disk space in /var or /home can cause your system to misbehave or stop services altogether. Monitor disk usage regularly.

Analyzing System Resource Consumption

Once you know what's being used, you'll want to identify who is using it. This is critical for troubleshooting and performance tuning.

Find High-CPU or High-Memory Processes

Using top or htop

Launch

```
$ top
```

Press P to sort by CPU.
Press M to sort by memory.
With htop, it's easier:

- Launch htop.
- Use F6 to sort by columns.

Using ps

List top memory users:

```
$ ps aux --sort=-%mem | head
USER        PID %CPU %MEM    VSZ   RSS TTY      STAT START   TIME COMMAND
mysql      1234 12.3 20.5 123456 23456 ?        Ssl  10:05   5:32 /usr/sbin/mysqld
```

- %MEM: Percentage of memory used
- %CPU: CPU usage

Tip Look at RSS (Resident Set Size); it shows actual RAM used.

Monitor Disk IO per Process with iotop

Install:

```
$ sudo apt install iotop
```

Run

```
$ sudo iotop
Total DISK READ: 1.23 M/s | Total DISK WRITE: 456.00 K/s
  TID  PRIO USER     DISK READ  DISK WRITE  SWAPIN     IO>    COMMAND
 1234 be/4 mysql     102.00 K/s  204.00 K/s  0.00 %   0.50 %  mysqld
```

Tip If a single process is writing too much, it may cause system slowdown, especially on HDDs or older SSDs.

Troubleshooting and Prerequisites for iotop and Related Tools

- Tools like **iotop** require **root privileges** (run with sudo) and specific kernel features enabled (e.g., CONFIG_TASK_DELAY_ACCT) to function properly.

- If iotop shows no output or fails silently, verify your kernel configuration and permissions.

- On some systems, **netstat** is deprecated or missing; consider using the modern alternative **ss** for socket statistics.

- Install any missing dependencies or packages (iotop depends on python and python3 utilities on some distros).

Managing System Logs

Logs are your best friends when troubleshooting issues or tracking performance history. Almost everything in Linux logs somewhere, especially in the /var/log directory.

Overview of Log Files (/var/log)

The directory /var/log contains the core logs of the system. Let's explore the most important ones.

/var/log/syslog: System Messages (Debian/Ubuntu)

Contains general system activity logs from various services.

```
$ less /var/log/syslog
Aug 08 14:22:03 myhost systemd[1]: Starting Daily apt download activities...
Aug 08 14:22:03 myhost systemd[1]: Finished Daily apt download activities.
```

Use tail for real-time viewing of logs:

```
$ tail -f /var/log/syslog
```

/var/log/messages: System Messages (RHEL/CentOS)

This file contains general system messages and is similar in purpose to /var/log/syslog on Debian-based systems. It's commonly used to review boot issues, kernel events, hardware errors, and other critical logs.

For authentication and security events on **RHEL/CentOS/AlmaLinux/Rocky**, check

```
$ sudo less /var/log/secure
Aug 08 14:30:01 myhost sudo:      user1 : TTY=pts/1 ; PWD=/home/user1 ;
USER=root ; COMMAND=/bin/lsAug 08 14:32:12 myhost sshd[1345]: Failed
password for root from 192.168.1.5 port 53212
```

> **Note** On **Debian/Ubuntu**, the equivalent file is /var/log/auth.log.

/var/log/kern.log: Kernel Logs

Logs directly from the Linux kernel (important for hardware and driver issues).

```
$ less /var/log/kern.log
```

/var/log/dmesg: Boot and Hardware Logs

Kernel ring buffer (also hardware detection during boot).

```
$ dmesg | less
[    0.000000] Linux version 5.15.0-88-generic ...
[    1.020000] usb 1-1: new high-speed USB device number 2
```

/var/log/apt/: Package Management Logs

Track what was installed, upgraded, or removed.

```
$ ls /var/log/apt/
history.log  term.log
```

To view:

```
$ less /var/log/apt/history.log
```

Tips for Viewing Logs

- cat: Prints the whole file.
- less: Scroll and search interactively.
- tail: Shows last lines (add -f to follow live).
- grep: Filters for keywords.

Example:

```
$ grep "error" /var/log/syslog
```

Using journalctl (for systemd-Based Systems)

Modern Linux distros (Ubuntu 20+, RHEL 7+, Debian 8+) use systemd, which collects logs via the journald daemon. Use journalctl to access them.

View All Logs

```
$ journalctl
```

Logs from a Specific Service

```
$ journalctl -u ssh
Aug 08 14:21:03 myhost systemd[1]: Started OpenSSH server daemon.
Aug 08 14:23:44 myhost sshd[1489]: Accepted password for user1 from 192.168.1.5
```

Logs from the Current Boot

```
$ journalctl -b
```

Real-Time Logs (like tail -f)

```
$ journalctl -f
```

Show Errors and Explanations

```
$ journalctl -xe
```

This is great for debugging service failures.

Rotating and Cleaning Logs

Logs can grow over time and fill up your disk. Linux handles this with log rotation.

Log Rotation with logrotate

logrotate manages automatic rotation, compression, and cleanup of log files to prevent disk space issues and keep logs manageable.

What It Does

- Rotates logs on a schedule (daily, weekly, etc.)
- Compresses old logs to save space
- Deletes or archives logs after a defined age
- Creates new empty log files as needed

```
Global config:$ cat /etc/logrotate.conf
Weekly
rotate 4
compress
create
include /etc/logrotate.d
```

> **Note** Most Linux distributions include the directory /etc/logrotate.d/ via this include directive.
>
> This allows individual packages (like rsyslog, nginx, mysql, etc.) to drop their own rotation rules into that directory—keeping the system modular and easier to manage.

Dry Run (Debug Mode)

You can test your configuration without making changes by using the **debug** flag:

`$ logrotate -d /etc/logrotate.conf`

This simulates what logrotate would do, showing output without rotating any files—helpful when testing new rules or troubleshooting.

Manually Rotate Logs

You can manually force a rotation:

`$ sudo logrotate /etc/logrotate.conf`

Explanation:

- logrotate reads the configuration file at /etc/logrotate.conf.
- It processes all the log rotation rules specified there, including any files referenced via include directives (like /etc/logrotate.d/).
- If any logs meet the criteria for rotation (e.g., size, date, etc.), it will rotate them (e.g., compress old logs, move logs, create new ones).
- If nothing needs to be rotated, it quietly exits.

To See What logrotate Is Doing, Add -v (Verbose) or -d (Debug)

`$ sudo logrotate -v /etc/logrotate.conf`

This will output detailed steps about which logs are being considered and what actions are being taken.

Identifying and Resolving Performance Bottlenecks

Now let's look at how to find what's slowing down your system, whether it's CPU, memory, disk IO, or networking.

Identifying High-Resource Processes

CPU/Memory Hogs with htop

```
$ htop
```

Sort by

- CPU: Press F6, and then choose %CPU.
- Memory: Choose %MEM.

Disk IO Hogs with iotop

```
$ sudo apt install iotop
$ sudo iotop
Total DISK READ: 1.2 MB/s | Total DISK WRITE: 3.4 MB/s
  TID  USER   DISK READ  DISK WRITE  COMMAND
 1234  mysql  1.1 MB/s   3.3 MB/s    mysqld
```

Network Usage

Check which ports/services are listening:

```
$ sudo netstat -tuln
```

Or better (modern):

```
$ sudo ss -tuln
Netid State   Recv-Q Send-Q Local Address:Port  Peer Address:Port
tcp   LISTEN  0      128    0.0.0.0:22          0.0.0.0:*
tcp   LISTEN  0      100    127.0.0.1:3306      0.0.0.0:*
tcp6  LISTEN  0      128    [::]:22             [::]:*
```

Explanation:

- Port 22: This is typically SSH, listening on all IPv4 and IPv6 interfaces.
- Port 3306: This is usually MySQL, listening only on 127.0.0.1 (localhost), meaning it only accepts local connections.
- Recv-Q/Send-Q: Queues of received/sent packets waiting to be processed.

Performance Optimization Tips

Disable Unused Services

List running services:

```
$ systemctl list-units --type=service
UNIT                        LOAD   ACTIVE SUB     DESCRIPTION
ssh.service                 loaded active running OpenBSD Secure Shell server
cron.service                loaded active running Regular background program
                                                  processing daemon
bluetooth.service           loaded active running Bluetooth service
networking.service          loaded active exited  Raise network interfaces
systemd-journald.service    loaded active running Journal Service
systemd-logind.service      loaded active running Login Service
...
```

Stop and disable a service:

```
$ sudo systemctl stop bluetooth
$ sudo systemctl disable bluetooth
```

Removed /etc/systemd/system/bluetooth.target.wants/bluetooth.service.

Clean Temporary Files

Install BleachBit:

```
$ sudo apt install bleachbit
```

Run BleachBit as root (to clean system files):

```
$ sudo bleachbit
```

Steps:

1. A window will open.
2. Check the boxes for what you want to clean (e.g., system cache, browser data).
3. Click **Preview** to see what will be deleted.
4. Then click **Clean**.

Clean Manually

Temporary files can build up over time and consume disk space. While you *can* delete them manually, it's important to proceed with caution.

Warning: Manual Deletion Can Be Risky

Commands like sudo rm -rf /tmp/* or /var/tmp/* can cause serious problems if used incorrectly, such as deleting important or in-use files or suffering from shell expansion errors.

If You Must Manually Clean (Proceed with Extreme Caution)

Instead of rm -rf, which can be dangerous, use find with safer options to avoid deleting critical directories:

```
$ sudo find /tmp -mindepth 1 -delete
$ sudo find /var/tmp -mindepth 1 -delete
```

This deletes contents of /tmp and /var/tmp without removing the directories themselves.

Safer Alternatives for Cleaning Temporary Files

On Debian/Ubuntu

Use the dedicated tool **tmpreaper**, which safely removes old files based on configurable policies:

```
$ sudo apt install tmpreaper
$ sudo tmpreaper [options] /tmp
```

On RHEL/CentOS/Fedora/AlmaLinux/Rocky

Use **systemd-tmpfiles**, which manages temporary files according to system policies defined in /usr/lib/tmpfiles.d/ and /etc/tmpfiles.d/:

```
$ sudo systemd-tmpfiles --clean
```

This is the preferred and default method on RHEL-family systems. While older tools like tmpwatch exist, they are mostly deprecated.

Adjust Swappiness

Swappiness controls how often Linux swaps RAM to disk.

Check the current value:

```
$ cat /proc/sys/vm/swappiness
60
```

Temporarily set to 10:

```
$ sudo sysctl vm.swappiness=10
vm.swappiness = 10
```

To make it permanent:

```
$ sudo nano /etc/sysctl.conf
```

Add

```
vm.swappiness=10
```

Use Lighter Desktop Environments

If you're running a GUI and want better performance:

- Switch from GNOME/KDE to XFCE, LXQt, or MATE.
- This reduces RAM usage compared with GNOME/KDE.

CHAPTER 7   SYSTEM MONITORING AND PERFORMANCE

Tuning System Parameters

Increase File Descriptors

File descriptors represent the number of files, sockets, and pipes a process can open. Many server applications (like databases and web servers) need higher limits.

Check the current value:

```
$ ulimit -n
1024
```

Increase by editing

```
$ sudo nano /etc/security/limits.conf
```

Add

```
* soft nofile 65535
* hard nofile 65535
```

This applies to **user sessions started through PAM** (e.g., interactive logins or su -), but **not** to services started via systemd.

For systemd Services: Use LimitNOFILE=

To raise the limit for a systemd-managed service (e.g., nginx, postgresql, etc.), you must configure it separately.

Create a Drop-In Override

```
$ sudo systemctl edit <service-name>
```

This opens a blank override file. Add

```
[Service]
LimitNOFILE=65535
```

Reload systemd and restart the service:

```
$ sudo systemctl daemon-reexec
$ sudo systemctl restart <service-name>
```

This ensures the service picks up the new file descriptor limit.

Importance of Increasing the File Descriptor Limit (ulimit -n)

Increasing the file descriptor limit allows the system to handle more simultaneous open files and network connections. This is crucial for high-performance servers like web servers, databases, and application backends, which can quickly exceed the default limit (usually 1,024).

Without raising it, applications may encounter "Too many open files" errors, leading to dropped connections or crashes under heavy load. Raising the limit improves system scalability and stability, especially for high-concurrency or I/O-intensive workloads.

TCP Network Performance Tweaks

Tuning TCP parameters can improve performance on systems handling high connection loads—especially web servers, proxies, or load balancers.

Reduce Stale TCP Connections and Improve Backlog Handling

Temporarily apply settings:

```
$ sudo sysctl -w net.core.somaxconn=1024
$ sudo sysctl -w net.ipv4.tcp_tw_reuse=1
```

These commands adjust

- net.core.somaxconn: Increases the maximum number of queued incoming connections (listen backlog)
- net.ipv4.tcp_tw_reuse: Allows reuse of sockets in TIME_WAIT state for **outgoing** connections

Caution: About net.ipv4.tcp_tw_reuse

This setting is **not a general-purpose TCP optimization** and should only be used when all of the following apply:

- Your system makes **many short-lived outgoing TCP connections** (e.g., HTTP clients, scrapers, API call loops).
- You **understand the networking context** of your application.

- You have **TCP timestamps enabled** (net.ipv4.tcp_timestamps = 1)—a kernel requirement for reuse logic.

- You're aware that **newer kernels** (e.g., Linux 4.12 and later) often restrict reuse behavior to **loopback interfaces** only.

Do not enable this on servers primarily accepting **inbound** TCP connections (e.g., web servers, databases). It won't help—and could interfere with TCP state tracking or NAT behavior.

For more technical context, see

- Linux man pages—tcp(7)

- Red Hat Performance Tuning Guide

Make Settings Persistent

To apply these values on boot, use a drop-in config file:

```
$ sudo nano /etc/sysctl.d/99-custom-tcp.conf
```

Add

```
net.core.somaxconn = 1024
net.ipv4.tcp_tw_reuse = 1
```

Apply immediately:

```
$ sudo sysctl --system
```

> **Tip** Use /etc/sysctl.d/*.conf instead of editing /etc/sysctl.conf directly. It's modular, easier to manage, and works better with package updates.

Importance of TCP Network Performance Tweaks

Tuning TCP parameters helps improve how the system handles incoming network connections, especially under high load.

- net.core.somaxconn = 1024 increases the size of the connection queue for pending TCP connections. This prevents dropped

CHAPTER 7 SYSTEM MONITORING AND PERFORMANCE

connections when many clients connect at once, which is essential for web servers, proxies, or API services.

- net.ipv4.tcp_tw_reuse = 1 allows the system to more quickly reuse TCP connections in the TIME_WAIT state. This reduces the number of stale or half-closed connections, improving performance and reducing port exhaustion in high-traffic environments.

Together, these tweaks improve responsiveness and reliability for network-heavy applications.

Long-Term Monitoring Tools

Glances (terminal-based) (See Figure 7-1):

```
$ sudo apt install glances
$ glances
```

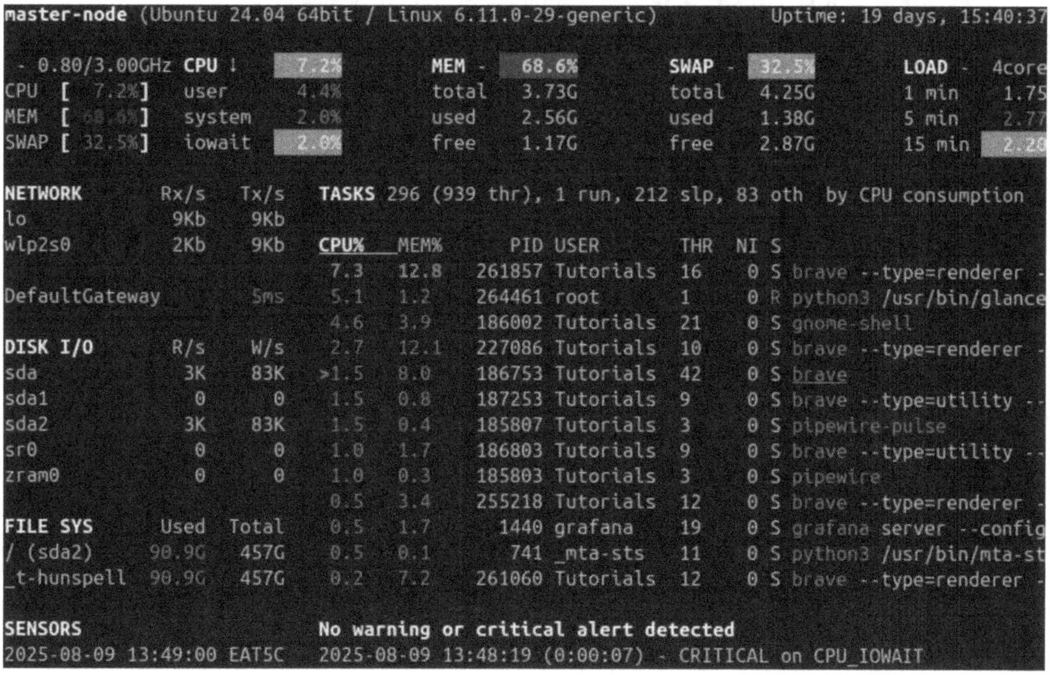

Figure 7-1. Interactive terminal view showing CPU, RAM, disk IO, etc

CHAPTER 7   SYSTEM MONITORING AND PERFORMANCE

Netdata (Dashboard via the Web)

Install Netdata using the official one-line installation script:

```
$ bash <(curl -SsL https://my-netdata.io/kickstart.sh)
Welcome to Netdata!
Checking dependencies...
Installing Netdata...
...
You can access Netdata at: http://localhost:19999/
```

For the latest installation instructions, refer to the official Netdata documentation: https://learn.netdata.cloud/docs/agent/packaging/installer.

Security note   By default, Netdata is accessible to anyone who knows the server's IP and the port (19999). To secure access:

- **Restrict access** using a firewall (e.g., ufw, iptables).
- **Set up a reverse proxy** with authentication (e.g., via Nginx).
- **Use Netdata Cloud** for secure remote monitoring and access control.

Access the Web Dashboard

After installation, Netdata runs as a background service and serves a real-time dashboard on port 19999.

Open in a Browser

If you're on the same machine (with a desktop environment), go to

```
$ http://localhost:19999
```

If you're accessing it remotely (e.g., via SSH):
Find your server's IP:

```
$ ip a | grep inet
```

Then go to

```
http://<your-server-ip>:19999
```

CHAPTER 7 SYSTEM MONITORING AND PERFORMANCE

Note Make sure port 19999 is open in your firewall or security group settings if you're accessing it from another machine.

What You'll See

Netdata's dashboard gives you real-time, interactive graphs, including

- CPU usage (per core + total)
- RAM and swap usage
- Disk IO
- Network traffic
- Processes, services, system load, etc.

Everything updates every second without needing a page refresh (See Figure 7-2).

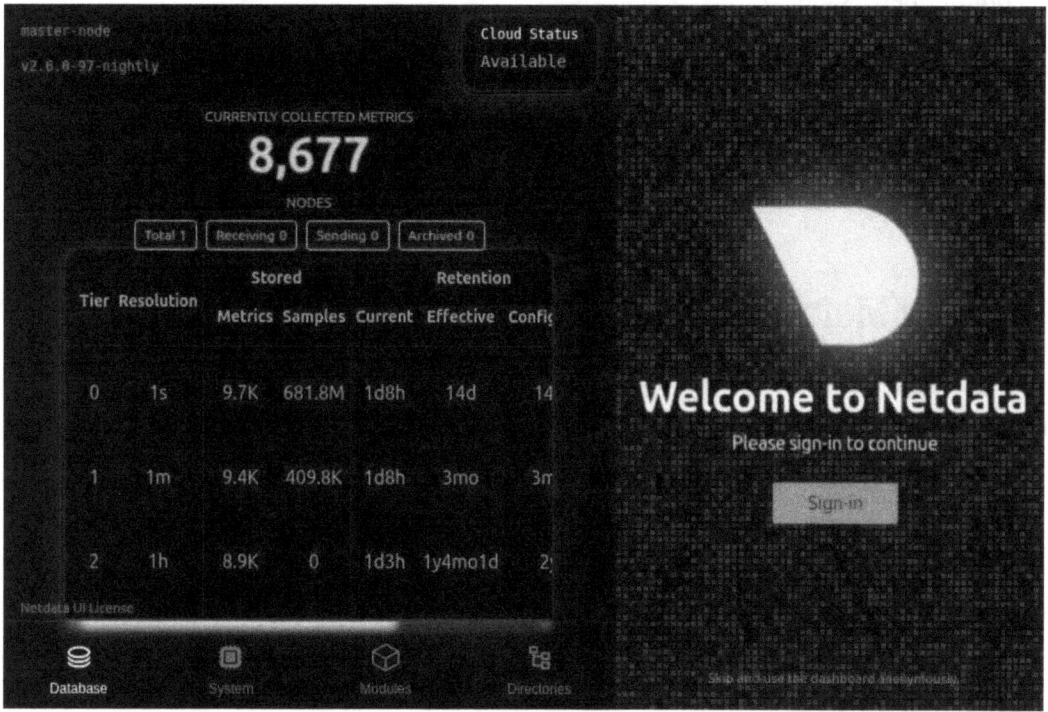

Figure 7-2. *Screenshot of a Netdata dashboard interface. On the left, it displays system metrics with a total of 8,677 currently collected metrics.*

Clarifications and Troubleshooting

iostat and sysstat: Immediate vs. Historical Usage

iostat is a command from the sysstat package that provides immediate, real-time statistics such as disk IO and CPU usage. You can run it immediately after installing sysstat.

Historical data collection with sar (also part of sysstat) requires enabling and starting the sysstat service or timer. This allows the system to collect metrics over time for later analysis.

netstat vs. ss: Which to Use?

netstat is part of the older net-tools package, which may not be installed by default on modern Linux systems.

ss, part of the iproute2 suite, is more efficient, actively maintained, and recommended as the modern replacement.

Example: List all listening TCP and UDP ports with ss:

```
$ ss -tuln
```

When you see netstat examples, verify if net-tools is installed or consider using ss instead.

Memory Metrics: "Used" vs. "Available"

The "available" memory metric shown by tools like free or vmstat is an estimate computed by the procps utilities and is not a direct kernel field. Older versions of procps may not display this column or might have inaccurate values.

Understanding this prevents misinterpretation of memory pressure, especially when "used" memory seems high but "available" shows free reclaimable memory.

iotop Prerequisites and Troubleshooting

iotop requires root privileges to access I/O statistics:

- Run with sudo iotop.

The kernel must have the following options enabled:

- CONFIG_TASK_DELAY_ACCT
- CONFIG_TASK_IO_ACCOUNTING
- CONFIG_TASKSTATS
- CONFIG_VM_EVENT_COUNTERS

For Linux kernel 5.14 and newer:

- Ensure kernel.task_delayacct=1 is set at boot or in /etc/sysctl.conf.

If iotop shows empty or no output, check kernel configs and permissions.

Linux Observability and Monitoring: Command Cheat Sheet

Task	Command	Notes/Distro Differences
Install htop Run htop	Debian/Ubuntu: sudo apt install htop htop	RHEL/Fedora: sudo dnf install htop Interactive process viewer
Install vmstat Run vmstat (five samples every two seconds)	Pre-installed in most distros vmstat 2 5	Part of procps (Debian/Ubuntu) or procps-ng (RHEL) Displays CPU, memory, I/O stats
Install iostat (sysstat) Run iostat with extended stats	Debian/Ubuntu: sudo apt install sysstat iostat -xz 1 5	RHEL/Fedora: sudo dnf install sysstat Requires sysstat package; sysstat service only for sar
Install dstat Run dstat	Debian/Ubuntu: sudo apt install dstat dstat	RHEL/Fedora: May require EPEL repository Versatile resource stats
Install iotop Run iotop (requires sudo)	Debian/Ubuntu: sudo apt install iotop sudo iotop	RHEL/Fedora: sudo dnf install iotop Requires kernel task accounting features
View logs (Debian/Ubuntu)	less /var/log/syslog	Auth logs: /var/log/auth.log

(*continued*)

Task	Command	Notes/Distro Differences
View logs (RHEL/Fedora)	less /var/log/messages	Auth logs: /var/log/secure
View systemd logs	journalctl	Use -u <service> to filter by service
Network connections (modern)	ss -tuln	Preferred over deprecated netstat
Increase file descriptors (shell)	Edit /etc/security/limits.conf	Requires logout/login to apply
Increase file descriptors (services)	Add LimitNOFILE= in systemd unit file	Reload daemon and restart service
Clean temp files safely	sudo systemd-tmpfiles --clean	Safer alternative to rm -rf /tmp/*
Check TCP tuning parameters	sysctl net.ipv4.tcp_tw_reuse	Use cautiously, with warnings

Quick recap:

- Use tools like top, htop, vmstat, and iotop to monitor system resources.
- Regularly check logs in /var/log and using journalctl.
- Using journalctl (for systemd-based systems):
  - View recent logs: journalctl -xe
  - Filter by service: journalctl -u <service-name>
  - Limit by time: journalctl --since "1 hour ago"
- Rotate and clean logs to save disk space.
- Tune system performance by identifying resource hogs and adjusting parameters.

Conclusion

Monitoring and performance tuning may sound like advanced tasks, but even beginners can quickly get up to speed with the right tools and a basic understanding. Over time, you'll start to notice patterns and anticipate problems before they happen.

A well-monitored system is a healthy system. By regularly checking logs, watching resource usage, and tuning performance settings, you'll become a more confident and capable Linux administrator.

CHAPTER 8

Introduction to Security

Security is one of the most critical aspects of Linux system administration. Even the most efficient server is useless if it's vulnerable to attacks. As administrators, our role is not only to keep systems running but also to protect them from unauthorized access, data breaches, and misuse. In this chapter, we'll explore core security concepts, configure firewalls, and secure user authentication and authorization.

Basic Security Concepts

Security is about protecting assets, whether data, services, or systems, from unauthorized access, disruption, or destruction. The three foundational pillars of information security are encapsulated in the CIA Triad.

Confidentiality

Ensuring that only authorized users can access specific information.

Integrity

Ensuring that information is not altered or tampered with by unauthorized individuals.

Availability

Ensuring that information and systems are accessible to authorized users when needed.

Key Definitions

- Risk: The potential for loss or damage when a threat exploits a vulnerability
- Threat: A possible danger that might exploit a vulnerability to breach security
- Vulnerability: A weakness in the system that can be exploited

Tip Always perform risk assessments regularly to understand which vulnerabilities pose the greatest threat to your specific environment.

Security Principles

A few foundational security principles guide system administrators when designing and maintaining secure systems.

Least Privilege

Only give users and applications the minimum access rights they need to perform their tasks.

- Do not run applications as root unless absolutely necessary.
- Use sudo instead of logging in as root.

Note The fewer privileges an account has, the less damage it can cause if compromised.

Defense in Depth

Use multiple layers of security. If one layer fails, others can still protect the system:

- Firewalls
- Authentication mechanisms
- Intrusion detection systems
- Application-level security

Zero Trust

Trust no one, not even users inside your network, by default. Every access attempt must be verified.

- Validate every user, device, and connection.
- Segment your network.

Common Linux Security Tools

Linux offers a robust set of built-in and third-party tools for securing systems.

Popular Tools

- iptables/nftables: Packet filtering and firewall configuration
- firewalld/UFW: Simplified firewall management
- fail2ban: Blocks IPs that show malicious signs
- chkrootkit/rkhunter: Rootkit detection tools
- auditd: Logs and monitors system activities
- AppArmor/SELinux: Mandatory Access Control (MAC) systems

CHAPTER 8   INTRODUCTION TO SECURITY

Configuring Firewalls

A firewall is the first line of defense for controlling incoming and outgoing network traffic.

Introduction to iptables and firewalld

- iptables: Traditional firewall tool that works by defining packet filtering rules
- firewalld: A newer firewall management service that uses zones and is easier to configure

Most modern Linux distributions use different default firewall tools depending on the distro:

- RHEL/Fedora (default: firewalld)
- Ubuntu (default: UFW)
- Debian (varies)

Firewall Setup: Before You Start (iptables/nftables/firewalld)

- Keep an existing SSH session open (so you don't get locked out).
- Know your distro's default firewall tool: ufw (Ubuntu), firewalld (RHEL), etc.
- Allow SSH **before** setting default DROP policies.
- Back up current rules (if applicable):

```
sudo iptables-save > ~/iptables-backup.rules      # iptables
sudo nft list ruleset > ~/nftables-backup.conf    # nftables
```

Packet Filtering with iptables, nftables, and firewalld

Linux provides several tools for configuring packet filtering rules, primarily iptables, nftables, and higher-level interfaces like firewalld.

iptables (Legacy Firewall Tool)

iptables is a traditional firewall utility that allows you to define rules to allow or block network traffic. It manipulates netfilter rules directly and is still supported, but many modern Linux distributions are transitioning to nftables.

Basic iptables Example

To block all incoming traffic except SSH (port 22):

```
$ sudo iptables -P INPUT DROP
$ sudo iptables -A INPUT -p tcp --dport 22 -j ACCEPT
$ sudo iptables -A INPUT -m conntrack --ctstate ESTABLISHED,RELATED -j ACCEPT
```

> **Note** These rules are not persistent across reboots. To save them:
> - On Debian/Ubuntu:
> - sudo apt install iptables-persistent
> - sudo netfilter-persistent save
> - On RHEL/CentOS: use service iptables save (if legacy iptables is enabled)

nftables (Modern Replacement for iptables)

nftables is the modern replacement for iptables, offering better performance, a unified syntax, and improved rule management. Many distributions now default to nftables instead of iptables.

Example: Allow SSH traffic using nftables syntax:

```
$ sudo nft add table inet filter
$ sudo nft add chain inet filter input { type filter hook input priority 0 \; }
$ sudo nft add rule inet filter input ct state established,related accept
$ sudo nft add rule inet filter input tcp dport 22 accept
$ sudo nft add rule inet filter input drop
```

> **Note** These nftables rules work on Ubuntu (20.04+), RHEL 8/9, and CentOS 8+. On systems with firewalld (RHEL) or ufw (Ubuntu), disable those services first to avoid conflicts.

firewalld (Front End for nftables or iptables)

firewalld is a dynamic firewall manager that simplifies rule creation using **zones** and **services**. Under the hood, it uses either iptables or nftables, depending on your system's back end. firewalld is the default on **RHEL, CentOS, Fedora**, and some others.

Setting Up Basic Firewall Rules with firewalld

Check if firewalld is running:

```
$ sudo systemctl status firewalld
● firewalld.service - firewalld - dynamic firewall daemon
   Loaded: loaded (/usr/lib/systemd/system/firewalld.service; enabled; vendor preset: enabled)
   Active: active (running) since Mon 2025-08-11 10:00:00 UTC; 5min ago
     Docs: man:firewalld(1)
 Main PID: 1234 (firewalld)
    Tasks: 2 (limit: 1123)
   Memory: 20.0M
   CGroup: /system.slice/firewalld.service
           └─1234 /usr/bin/python3 /usr/sbin/firewalld --nofork --nopid
```

Start and enable it:

```
$ sudo systemctl start firewalld
$ sudo systemctl enable firewalld
```

Check the default zone:

```
$ sudo firewall-cmd --get-default-zone
public
```

CHAPTER 8 INTRODUCTION TO SECURITY

List active rules:

```
$ sudo firewall-cmd --list-all
public (active)
  target: default
  icmp-block-inversion: no
  interfaces: eth0
  sources:
  services: dhcpv6-client ssh
  ports:
  protocols:
  masquerade: no
  forward-ports:
  source-ports:
  icmp-blocks:
  rich rules:
```

Allowing and Blocking Ports

Allow HTTP (port 80):

```
$ sudo firewall-cmd --permanent --add-service=http
$ sudo firewall-cmd --reload
success
success
```

Allow HTTPS (port 443):

```
$ sudo firewall-cmd --permanent --add-service=https
$ sudo firewall-cmd --reload
success
success
```

Block a specific port (e.g., 8080):

```
$ sudo firewall-cmd --permanent --remove-port=8080/tcp
$ sudo firewall-cmd --reload
success
success
```

> **Note** The above commands only remove the existing rule allowing traffic on port 8080. This does **not** explicitly block the port unless your default firewall policy is set to deny or drop all other traffic.

To explicitly block a port in firewalld, you can use a **rich rule**, for example:

```
$ sudo firewall-cmd --permanent --add-rich-rule='rule family="ipv4" port port="8080" protocol="tcp" reject'
$ sudo firewall-cmd --reload
```

Alternatively, you can configure your firewall with a **default drop policy**, which means **all incoming connections are blocked by default**, except for the ports or services you explicitly allow. This approach simplifies firewall management by ensuring that any port not explicitly permitted is automatically blocked, improving overall security.

User Authentication and Authorization

Understanding Authentication Methods

Linux supports multiple authentication methods:

- Password-based: The most common method, but vulnerable if passwords are weak
- SSH key-based: More secure; requires generating a key pair
- Two-factor authentication (2FA): Adds an extra layer of security

Before You Start: SSH Hardening

- Open a second SSH session so you don't lose access if the config breaks.
- Make sure your non-root user has sudo privileges.

- Generate and test SSH key login **before** disabling password auth.
- Back up your SSH config:

    sudo cp /etc/ssh/sshd_config /etc/ssh/sshd_config.bak

Password-Based Authentication (Default Method)

This is the simplest and default way of connecting to a remote Linux server. You SSH into the server using a username and are prompted to enter a password for that user account:

$ ssh user@server_ip

If password authentication is enabled, you'll see

$ user@server_ip's password:

Once you enter the correct password, you're granted access.

Pros

- Easy to set up (no need to generate or install keys)
- Works by default on most Linux servers
- Familiar for beginners

Cons

- Easier to brute-force or guess, especially if weak passwords are used.
- Password reuse (e.g., using the same password across systems) increases risk.
- Vulnerable to keyloggers or phishing attacks.
- Shared user accounts with the same password can't be audited per user.

How to Use It (and Secure It)

Make sure password login is enabled (if not already) by editing

```
$ sudo nano /etc/ssh/sshd_config
```

Find or add

```
PasswordAuthentication yes
```

Restart the SSH service:
On **Debian/Ubuntu**:

```
$ sudo systemctl restart ssh
```

On **RHEL/Fedora/AlmaLinux/Rocky Linux**:

```
$ sudo systemctl restart sshd
```

Best Practices for Password-Based Login

If you choose to use password authentication, secure it properly.

Use strong passwords:

- At least 12 characters.
- Mix of uppercase and lowercase letters, numbers, and symbols.
- Avoid dictionary words or simple phrases.

Limit login attempts using Fail2Ban; we'll look at this topic later on to see how Fail2Ban can block IPs after repeated failures.

Lock out inactive accounts:

```
$ sudo passwd -l username
```

Disable root login:
Edit /etc/ssh/sshd_config:

```
PermitRootLogin no
```

Monitor failed login attempts:

```
$ sudo grep "Failed password" /var/log/auth.log
Aug 12 15:10:42 server sshd[2814]: Failed password for invalid user test
from 192.168.1.100 port 51234 ssh2
Aug 12 15:10:45 server sshd[2814]: Failed password for user from
192.168.1.100 port 51234 ssh2
```

Setting Up SSH Key Authentication

SSH key authentication is a secure method of logging into a remote Linux server without using a password. Instead, it uses asymmetric cryptography, a key pair consisting of

- Private key: Stored securely on your client machine (e.g., your laptop)
- Public key: Stored on the server in the user's account

Only someone with the matching private key can authenticate to the server that has the public key.

Why Use SSH Keys Instead of Passwords?

- Stronger than even complex passwords
- Not vulnerable to brute-force attacks
- Can be used with passphrases and two-factor authentication
- No need to remember or enter a password every time

Step-by-Step Guide: SSH Key Authentication

Generate a key pair on your client machine:

```
$ ssh-keygen -t rsa -b 4096

Generating public/private rsa key pair.
Enter file in which to save the key (/home/user/.ssh/id_rsa): [Press Enter]
Enter passphrase (empty for no passphrase):
Enter same passphrase again:
Your identification has been saved in /home/user/.ssh/id_rsa
```

CHAPTER 8   INTRODUCTION TO SECURITY

```
Your public key has been saved in /home/user/.ssh/id_rsa.pub
The key fingerprint is:
SHA256:abcdef1234567890xyz root@master-node
The key's randomart image is:
+---[RSA 4096]----+
| .+o+==+..       |
|. .o.o+= .       |
| + o +* o        |
| = +.+o          |
|. o .o S         |
|  . . .          |
|   E             |
+----[SHA256]-----+
```

Explanation:

- ssh-keygen: The command to generate SSH key pairs
- -t rsa: Specifies the type of key to generate (RSA)
- -b 4096: Sets the key length to 4,096 bits for strong encryption

After completion, two files are created:

- ~/.ssh/id_rsa: Your private key (keep this secret!)
- ~/.ssh/id_rsa.pub: Your public key (this will go on the server)

Copy the public key to your server:

Use ssh-copy-id to send your public key to the server. Replace user and server_ip with the actual values of your system.

```
$  sudo ssh-copy-id root@192.168.1.100

/usr/bin/ssh-copy-id: INFO: Source of key(s) to be installed: "/root/.ssh/id_rsa.pub"
/usr/bin/ssh-copy-id: INFO: attempting to log in with the new key(s), to filter out any that are already installed
root@192.168.1.100's password:
Number of key(s) added: 1
```

CHAPTER 8　INTRODUCTION TO SECURITY

Explanation:

- ssh-copy-id: Installs your public key in the server's ~/.ssh/authorized_keys file

- root@192.168.1.100: The username and IP address of the remote server

Test SSH Login Without a Password

Now you can log in securely using your key.

```
$ ssh ubuntu@192.168.1.100
Welcome to Ubuntu 22.04.1 LTS (GNU/Linux 5.15.0-84-generic x86_64)
Last login: Fri Aug 9 12:00:00 2025 from 192.168.1.10
root@server:~#
```

If you added a passphrase when generating the key, you'll be prompted for it. If not, you'll log in immediately, no password required.

Note　It is recommended to avoid logging in directly as root over SSH for security reasons. Instead, use a non-root user and perform administrative tasks with sudo.

Optional: Disable Password Authentication on the Server

To prevent password-based login entirely (for better security):
SSH into the server:

```
$ ssh user@server_ip
```

Open the SSH config file:

```
$ sudo nano /etc/ssh/sshd_config
```

Find and change these lines:

```
PasswordAuthentication no
KbdInteractiveAuthentication yes   # Or leave as default
UsePAM yes
```

179

Optional: If you want to use SSH keys only and combine with two-factor authentication (2FA), configure

AuthenticationMethods publickey,keyboard-interactive
PasswordAuthentication no

This setup is safer and aligns with modern OpenSSH best practices.
Restart the SSH service:
On **Debian/Ubuntu**:

```
$ sudo systemctl restart ssh
```

On **RHEL/Fedora/AlmaLinux/Rocky Linux**:

```
$ sudo systemctl restart sshd
```

Warning Make sure your key authentication works before disabling password logins, or you could lock yourself out of the server.

Set Up Two-Factor Authentication (2FA)
Before You Start: Enabling SSH 2FA

- Confirm SSH key–based login is working **before** enabling 2FA.
- Ensure sudo access with a non-root user.
- Keep a current SSH session active in case of misconfiguration.
- Back up your PAM and SSH configs:

```
sudo cp /etc/pam.d/sshd /etc/pam.d/sshd.bak
sudo cp /etc/ssh/sshd_config /etc/ssh/sshd_config.bak
```

Why Use 2FA?

If an attacker gets access to your SSH key or password, 2FA still blocks them without the second factor (usually a time-based code on your phone).

We'll use Google Authenticator, which is simple and widely supported.

Step-by-Step Setup

Install the Google Authenticator PAM Module

Ubuntu/Debian:

```
$ sudo apt install libpam-google-authenticator
```

RHEL/CentOS:

```
$ sudo dnf install google-authenticator
```

Run on Each User Account

Log in as the user (e.g., ubuntu) and run

```
$ google-authenticator
```

You'll see the following prompt:

```
Do you want authentication tokens to be time-based (y/n) y
```

A QR code appears:

```
Your new secret key is: ABCDEFGHIJKLMNOP
Your verification code is 123456
```

Your emergency scratch codes are

```
94812345
32987562
49817234
74329184
10394857
Do you want me to update your "/home/ubuntu/.google_authenticator"
file? (y/n) y
Do you want to disallow multiple uses of the same authentication
token? (y/n) y
By default, tokens are good for 30 seconds. In order to compensate for
possible time-skew between the client and the server,
we allow an extra token before and after the current time. Do you want to
do so? (y/n) n
```

CHAPTER 8   INTRODUCTION TO SECURITY

If the computer that you are logging into isn't hardened against brute-force login attempts,
you can enable rate-limiting for the authentication module. Do you want to enable rate-limiting? (y/n) y

Done! You'll see a QR code (scan with Google Authenticator app), a secret key, and backup codes.

Note on emergency scratch codes   Save them somewhere secure!

Edit PAM Configuration

Edit the SSH PAM file:

$ sudo nano /etc/pam.d/sshd

Add this at the top:

auth required pam_google_authenticator.so

Edit SSH Configuration

Open the SSH server config:

$ sudo nano /etc/ssh/sshd_config

Change or add the following:

ChallengeResponseAuthentication yes
PasswordAuthentication yes
UsePAM yes

Note   If you're using SSH keys only, set PasswordAuthentication no.

Restart SSH:

$ sudo systemctl restart ssh

Test SSH Login

Try logging in:

```
$ ssh ubuntu@192.168.1.100
Password:
Verification code: 582194
Welcome to Ubuntu 22.04.1 LTS (GNU/Linux 5.15.0-84-generic x86_64)
```

You'll now see:
Verification code, and it will change every 30 seconds in your Google Authenticator app.

Fail2Ban: Automatically Block Brute-Force Attacks

What Is Fail2Ban?

Fail2Ban is a daemon that monitors log files for suspicious behavior (like repeated failed login attempts) and then bans offending IP addresses via the firewall (iptables, UFW, etc.).

Step-by-Step Setup

Install Fail2Ban

Ubuntu/Debian:

```
$ sudo apt update
$ sudo apt install fail2ban
```

RHEL/CentOS:

```
$ sudo dnf install epel-release
$ sudo dnf install fail2ban
```

Create the Config File

Instead of copying the entire jail.conf, it's recommended to create a minimal override file /etc/fail2ban/jail.local with just the necessary settings. This helps your changes survive Fail2Ban updates:

```
$ sudo cp /etc/fail2ban/jail.conf /etc/fail2ban/jail.local
$ sudo nano /etc/fail2ban/jail.local
```

Add the following minimal configuration for the SSH jail, adjusting the log path based on your OS:

```
[sshd]
enabled = true
port = ssh
filter = sshd
maxretry = 5
bantime = 1h
findtime = 10m
logpath = /var/log/auth.log    # Use this on Debian/Ubuntu
# logpath = /var/log/secure    # Use this on RHEL/Fedora/AlmaLinux/
Rocky Linux
```

Explanation:

- enabled: Turns on the jail
- port: The SSH port (default is 22)
- filter: The filter to use (sshd for SSH)
- maxretry: Number of failed attempts before banning an IP (five)
- bantime: Duration of the ban (one hour)
- findtime: Time window to count failures (ten minutes)
- logpath: Path to the SSH authentication log (varies by OS)

Start and Enable Fail2Ban

```
$ sudo systemctl enable fail2ban
$ sudo systemctl start fail2ban
 Created symlink /etc/systemd/system/multi-user.target.wants/fail2ban.service → /lib/systemd/system/fail2ban.service.
```

Check Status

```
$ sudo fail2ban-client status sshd
```

```
Status for the jail: sshd
|- Filter
|  |- Currently failed: 0
|  |- Total failed: 12
|  `- File list: /var/log/auth.log
`- Actions
   |- Currently banned: 1
   |- Total banned: 2
   `- Banned IP list: 192.168.0.101
```

Unban an IP

```
$ sudo fail2ban-client set sshd unbanip 192.168.0.101
OK
```

Monitor Logins with auditd (Audit Daemon)

Why Use auditd?

auditd tracks every access and change to the system, including who logged in, from where, and what they did. Essential for forensics and compliance.

CHAPTER 8   INTRODUCTION TO SECURITY

Step-by-Step Setup

Install auditd:

```
$ sudo apt install auditd audispd-plugins
$ sudo dnf install audit audit-libs
```

Enable and start:

```
$ sudo systemctl enable auditd
$ sudo systemctl start auditd
 Created symlink /etc/systemd/system/multi-user.target.wants/auditd.service
→ /usr/lib/systemd/system/auditd.service.
```

Ensure auditd is running:

```
$ sudo systemctl status auditd
```

- auditd.service - Security Auditing Service
     Loaded: loaded (/usr/lib/systemd/system/auditd.service; enabled;
     preset: enabled)
     Active: active (running) since Tue 2025-08-12 20:16:19 EAT;
     3min 42s ago
       Docs: man:auditd(8)
             https://github.com/linux-audit/audit-documentation
   Main PID: 72651 (auditd)
      Tasks: 2 (limit: 4491)
     Memory: 912.0K (peak: 11.2M)
        CPU: 78ms
     CGroup: /system.slice/auditd.service
             └─72651 /sbin/auditd

Audit Login Events

To track all user login/logout events:

```
$ sudo ausearch -m USER_LOGIN
----
time->Tue Aug 12 10:15:22 2025
```

CHAPTER 8 INTRODUCTION TO SECURITY

```
type=USER_LOGIN msg=audit(1628763322.123:100): pid=1023 uid=0
auid=1000 ses=1 msg='op=login id=1000 exe="/usr/sbin/sshd" hostname=?
addr=192.168.0.55 terminal=ssh res=success'
```

You can also run

```
$ sudo aureport --login
Login Report
============================================================================
# date          time     acct      host           term     exe
success event
============================================================================
1. 12/08/2025  10:15:22 john      192.168.0.55  sshd     /usr/sbin/sshd
yes      100
```

This shows a nice summary of login attempts.

Audit SSH Config File Changes

Track changes to your SSH configuration:

Edit rules:

```
$ sudo nano /etc/audit/rules.d/ssh.rules
```

Add

```
-w /etc/ssh/sshd_config -p wa -k ssh_config
```

Reload rules:

```
$ sudo augenrules --load
Loaded rules from: /etc/audit/rules.d/ssh.rules
Rules successfully loaded
```

Search for changes:

```
$ sudo ausearch -k ssh_config
----
time->Tue Aug 13 11:07:33 2025
```

CHAPTER 8 INTRODUCTION TO SECURITY

```
type=CONFIG_CHANGE msg=audit(1691921253.123:101): auid=1000 uid=0 gid=0
ses=5 subj==unconfined_u:unconfined_r:unconfined_t:s0-s0:c0.c1023
op=updated rules /etc/ssh/sshd_config key=ssh_config
----
time->Tue Aug 13 11:09:44 2025
type=PATH msg=audit(1691921384.456:102): item=0 name="/etc/ssh/sshd_config"
inode=134579 dev=08:01 mode=0100644 ouid=0 ogid=0 rdev=00:00 obj=unconfined
_u:object_r:etc_t:s0 nametype=NORMAL
```

View Audit Log

```
$ cat /var/log/audit/audit.log
type=SYSCALL msg=audit(1691921200.789:99): arch=c000003e syscall=2
success=yes exit=3 a0=7ffddc3c3c10 a1=241 a2=1b6 a3=0 items=1 ppid=1234
pid=4321 auid=1000 uid=0 gid=0 euid=0 suid=0 fsuid=0 egid=0 ...
```

For readable analysis, use

```
$ sudo ausearch -k ssh_config
$ sudo aureport
```

Optional: Restrict SSH Access by IP Address

If you manage SSH for a known group (e.g., office or your home IP), you can lock access to trusted IPs only.

Restrict SSH Access Using UFW

Allow from a specific IP:

```
$ sudo ufw allow from 203.0.113.50 to any port 22
Rule added
```

CHAPTER 8   INTRODUCTION TO SECURITY

Important   Ensure that the specific **ALLOW** rule for your trusted IP exists alongside a **default deny** policy for other traffic on port 22. Because UFW evaluates more specific rules before generic ones, the order and specificity of rules matter, especially if you mix specific **ALLOW** and **DENY** rules for the same port.

Deny All Other SSH

```
$ sudo ufw deny 22/tcp
Rule added
```

Check Status

```
$ sudo ufw status verbose

Status: active
To                         Action      From
--                         ------      ----
22/tcp                     DENY        Anywhere
22                         ALLOW       203.0.113.50
22/tcp (v6)                DENY        Anywhere (v6)
```

Understanding AppArmor and SELinux (MAC Systems)

What Is MAC (Mandatory Access Control)?

Before diving into AppArmor or SELinux individually, let's understand Mandatory Access Control.

MAC vs. DAC

Access Control Type	Description
DAC (Discretionary Access Control)	Traditional Unix/Linux model (file owners set chmod, chown, etc.).
MAC (Mandatory Access Control)	Access is controlled by policies enforced by the system, not just user permissions.

In short:

- DAC lets users set their own rules.
- MAC forces strict system-defined rules; even root can be restricted.

SELinux: Security-Enhanced Linux

What Is SELinux?

SELinux is a MAC framework originally developed by the NSA and now maintained by Red Hat. It's widely used in RHEL, CentOS, Fedora, and even Android.

It uses labels, contexts, and policies to decide what each process is allowed to do.

SELinux Modes

Check the current mode:

```
$ getenforce
```

You'll see one of the modes shown in Table 8-1.

Table 8-1. SELinux Operational Modes

Mode	Description
Enforcing	SELinux policies are enforced (active protection).
Permissive	Logs violations but doesn't block (used for testing).
Disabled	SELinux is turned off.

Change the SELinux mode temporarily:

```
$ sudo setenforce 0
$ sudo setenforce 1
```

Change the mode permanently:

```
$ sudo nano /etc/selinux/config
```

Set one of

```
SELINUX=enforcing
SELINUX=permissive
SELINUX=disabled
```

How SELinux Works: Concepts

Type enforcement (TE): Every file, process, and user is labeled with a type.

Contexts: They look like this:

```
system_u:object_r:httpd_sys_content_t:s0
User: system_u
Role: object_r
Type: httpd_sys_content_t (used by Apache web server)
```

Basic SELinux Commands

Check file contexts:

```
$ ls -Z /var/www/html
-rw-r--r--. root root system_u:object_r:httpd_sys_content_t:s0 index.html
```

Change the file label:

```
$ sudo chcon -t httpd_sys_content_t /var/www/html/index.html
```

View the process context:

```
$ ps -eZ | grep httpd
system_u:system_r:httpd_t:s0      1234 ? 00:00:01 httpd
system_u:system_r:httpd_t:s0      1235 ? 00:00:00 httpd
```

CHAPTER 8 INTRODUCTION TO SECURITY

Restore default contexts:

```
$ sudo restorecon -Rv /var/www/html
restorecon reset /var/www/html/index.html context
system_u:object_r:default_t:s0->system_u:object_r:httpd_sys_content_t:s0
```

Fix the 403 Error with SELinux

You place your website files in /srv/www, but Apache returns a 403 Forbidden. Why?
Because SELinux only allows Apache to read files with the httpd_sys_content_t type.
Fix:

```
$ sudo chcon -R -t httpd_sys_content_t /srv/www
```

Or better:

```
$ sudo semanage fcontext -a -t httpd_sys_content_t "/srv/www(/.*)?"
$ sudo restorecon -Rv /srv/www
```

View SELinux Logs

SELinux violations are logged here:

```
/var/log/audit/audit.log
```

Check for recent denials:

```
$ sudo ausearch -m avc -ts recent
type=AVC msg=audit(1689392400.123:456): avc:  denied  { read }
for  pid=7890 comm="httpd" name="index.html" dev="sda1" ino=123456 scontext
=system_u:system_r:httpd_t:s0 tcontext=unconfined_u:object_r:user_home_t:s0
tclass=file
```

Install GUI Tools (Optional for Testing)

Fedora/RHEL:

```
$ sudo dnf install policycoreutils-gui
```

AppArmor: Application Armor

What Is AppArmor?

AppArmor is another MAC system used mainly in Debian, Ubuntu, and SUSE. It's easier to manage than SELinux and uses path-based access control instead of labels.

- Easier to configure.
- Profiles are assigned to binaries.
- Denies access outside explicitly allowed paths.

Check AppArmor Status

```
$ sudo aa-status
apparmor module is loaded.
30 profiles are loaded.
27 profiles are in enforce mode.
3 profiles are in complain mode.
0 processes have profiles defined.
```

How AppArmor Works

Each program (like /usr/sbin/nginx) gets a profile stored in

/etc/apparmor.d/

Example profile:

/etc/apparmor.d/usr.sbin.nginx

These profiles specify what files the process can read/write, what network actions it can take, and more.

Enable/Disable Profiles

Enable:

```
$ sudo aa-enforce /etc/apparmor.d/usr.sbin.nginx
```

Disable:

```
$ sudo aa-disable /etc/apparmor.d/usr.sbin.nginx
```

Put into Complain Mode

```
$ sudo aa-complain /etc/apparmor.d/usr.sbin.nginx
```

Edit AppArmor Profiles

You can create or edit profiles using

```
$ sudo aa-genprof /usr/sbin/nginx
Profile generation for /usr/sbin/nginx
Please read the profile and decide on the permissions
...
(press Enter to continue, etc.)
```

This tool walks you through defining a new profile.

To update an existing one:

```
$ sudo aa-logprof
Reading AppArmor log entries and updating profiles
```

Found denied entries:

```
[1] /usr/sbin/nginx tried to read /etc/nginx/nginx.conf
Allow this access? (y/n)
```

This reads from the log and helps update policies based on denied actions.

Profile Location

All AppArmor profiles are in

/etc/apparmor.d/

View AppArmor Logs

Logged to

/var/log/syslog

Or filter for AppArmor:

```
$ sudo dmesg | grep apparmor
[ 1234.567890] audit: type=1400 audit(1689392400.123:456): apparmor="DENIED" operation="open" profile="/usr/sbin/nginx" name="/etc/nginx/nginx.conf" pid=7890 comm="nginx" requested_mask="r" denied_mask="r" fsuid=0 ouid=0
```

Which One Should You Use?

Use AppArmor if

- You're on Ubuntu/Debian and want quick and simple protection.
- You're new to MAC systems.
- You want a readable, file-based policy system.

Use SELinux if

- You're on Red Hat/Fedora/CentOS.
- You need strict security in production.
- You're deploying regulated systems (e.g., HIPAA, PCI).

Note You can't (and shouldn't) use both on the same system. Stick to the one native to your distro.

Real-World Scenario: Hardening a Web Server

Let's say you're running nginx on Ubuntu. Here's a mini checklist:

Ensure AppArmor is active:

```
$ sudo aa-status
```

Make sure nginx has an enforced profile:

```
$ sudo aa-enforce /etc/apparmor.d/usr.sbin.nginx
```

Test nginx, if denied actions are logged:

```
$ sudo aa-logprof
```

Limit file access only to

/var/www/html/
/etc/nginx/

Monitor logs for denials:

```
$ sudo dmesg | grep apparmor
```

chkrootkit/rkhunter: Rootkit Detection Tools

A rootkit is a collection of tools or code that enables attackers to

- Hide their presence on the system.
- Escalate privileges (gain root access).
- Log keystrokes or steal data.
- Launch backdoors for later access.

Rootkits are particularly dangerous because they operate at the kernel or system level, remaining invisible to normal tools like ps, ls, or top.

How to Detect Rootkits on Linux

That's where tools like chkrootkit and rkhunter come in, they scan for traces of common rootkits by looking for

- Known rootkit files
- Suspicious binaries or symlinks
- Modified system commands (ls, netstat, etc.)
- Hidden processes, network connections, or users

chkrootkit

What Is chkrootkit?

chkrootkit is a lightweight shell script that uses common Linux tools (ls, ps, ifconfig, etc.) to search for rootkits.

It scans

- Common system binaries for changes
- Hidden directories
- Signs of known rootkits

Installation

On Ubuntu/Debian

```
$ sudo apt install chkrootkit
```

On RHEL/CentOS

```
$ sudo dnf install chkrootkit
```

Run the scan:

```
$ sudo chkrootkit
```

You'll get output like

```
Checking `amd'... not found
Checking `basename'... not infected
Checking `biff'... not infected
...
```

If a suspicious item is found:

```
Checking `ssh'... INFECTED
```

To scan a specific directory:

```
$ sudo chkrootkit -r /path/to/mounted/system
```

Useful if you're scanning a mounted disk image or backup.

> **Note** chkrootkit can return false positives. Use logs and manual checks to confirm. Always check the official rootkit list: /usr/lib/chkrootkit.

rkhunter (Rootkit Hunter)

What Is rkhunter?

rkhunter is a more advanced tool that scans for rootkits, backdoors, and suspicious system changes.
   It

- Checks file hashes against known good ones
- Scans for hidden files, suspicious permissions, and malicious strings
- Logs everything clearly and verbosely

Installation

On Ubuntu/Debian

```
$ sudo apt install rkhunter
```

On RHEL/CentOS

```
$ sudo dnf install epel-release
$ sudo dnf install rkhunter
```

Update Before Scanning

To get the latest rootkit definitions and known good hashes:

```
$ sudo rkhunter --update
rkhunter update started at Thu Aug 13 10:00:00 2025
Checking rkhunter data files...
    Checking file mirrors.dat                              [ Update found ]
    Checking file programs_bad.dat                         [ Update found ]
    Checking file backdoorports.dat                        [ Update found ]
    Checking file suspscan.dat                             [ Update found ]
```

Downloading updates...
Update data files downloaded successfully.

```
$ sudo rkhunter --propupd
Propupd started at Thu Aug 13 10:05:00 2025
The file properties database has been updated.
```

--propupd creates a baseline database of your current system files (first-time only).

Run a Full Scan

```
$ sudo rkhunter --check
Checking system commands...
Checking for rootkits...
Checking for hidden files and directories...
Checking for suspicious strings...
Checking for writable files and directories...
Checking for malware infections...
Checking for local exploits...
Checking for trojans...
Checking for backdoors...
Checking for default passwords...
Scan completed. No rootkits found.
```

View the log:

```
$ sudo less /var/log/rkhunter.log
[Rootkit Hunter Version 1.4.6]
Checking system commands...
Checking for rootkits...
Checking for hidden files and directories...
Warning: Suspect file found: /usr/bin/suspicious
Scan results: No rootkits found
```

Tip Use /WARNING or /INFECTED in less to jump to red flags.

Optional: Run Daily with cron

Add to /etc/cron.daily/rkhunter:

```
#!/bin/bash
/usr/bin/rkhunter --update
/usr/bin/rkhunter --check --cronjob --report-warnings-only
```

Make it executable:

```
$ sudo chmod +x /etc/cron.daily/rkhunter
```

Best Practices for Rootkit Detection

- Run scans regularly (daily or weekly) using cron.
- Update signature databases frequently.
- Set a known good baseline (with rkhunter --propupd) after a clean install.

Monitor logs for anomalies:

```
$ sudo less /var/log/rkhunter.log
$ sudo grep "INFECTED" /var/log/chkrootkit.log
```

- Combine with
- Audit logging (auditd)
- Fail2Ban
- AppArmor or SELinux
- Tripwire or AIDE for file integrity checks

What to Do If You Suspect a Rootkit?

- Immediately disconnect the system from the network.
- Boot into rescue mode or from a live CD.

- Mount the filesystem read-only and copy logs (/var/log) for offline inspection.

- Run rootkit detection tools from outside the affected OS.

- If confirmed, consider a full reinstall; you can't trust a compromised system.

Conclusion

Security is not a one-time setup but a continuous process. By understanding threats, applying least privilege, using firewalls, and strengthening authentication, we create a robust foundation for protecting our Linux systems.

CHAPTER 9

Networking and Remote Access

Linux system administration is not complete without understanding networking and remote access. Whether you're managing a server, configuring a client, or setting up remote management tools, knowing how to configure networks and access systems remotely is essential.

This chapter will guide you through

- Hostname and DNS configuration
- Editing network configuration files
- Troubleshooting networking issues
- Setting up SSH for secure remote access
- Understanding and configuring VPNs (Virtual Private Networks)
- Using SCP and SFTP for secure file transfers

Hostname and DNS Configuration

When you connect to a network, whether it's your home Wi-Fi, a corporate LAN, or the internet, your system needs two key things to communicate:

1. A hostname—a unique name that identifies your computer on the network
2. A way to resolve domain names to IP addresses, typically using DNS (Domain Name System)

Let's break down what this all means and how to configure it properly.

Setting the Hostname

Every Linux machine has a hostname; it's the name it uses to introduce itself on the network. You might have seen it show up in your terminal prompt:

user@my-linux-box:~$

In this case, my-linux-box is the hostname.

Changing the Hostname

In modern Linux distributions that use systemd, you can change the hostname using the hostnamectl command.

To set a new hostname:

```
$ sudo hostnamectl set-hostname my-new-hostname
```

Replace my-new-hostname with whatever you want. Just keep it simple—avoid spaces or special characters.

To view your current hostname:

```
$ hostnamectl
   Static hostname: master-node
         Icon name: computer-laptop
           Chassis: laptop
        Machine ID: 332a080d9002483da27e01c5ece55cb3
           Boot ID: 71c8878a44a445c486fe184ae63c158f
  Operating System: Ubuntu 24.04.2 LTS
            Kernel: Linux 6.14.0-27-generic
      Architecture: x86-64
   Hardware Vendor: Dell Inc.
    Hardware Model: Latitude E5540
  Firmware Version: A06
     Firmware Date: Thu 2014-05-01
      Firmware Age: 11y 3month 2w
```

Editing /etc/hosts and /etc/resolv.conf

The hostnamectl command changes your system hostname, but that's only one part of the picture. Your system also uses two important files for name resolution:

- /etc/hosts
- /etc/resolv.conf

Let's see what these do.

/etc/hosts: Local Name Mapping

Before your system queries external DNS servers, it checks the /etc/hosts file for hostname-to-IP address mappings. This allows local name resolution without needing to contact a DNS server.

Here's an example of a typical /etc/hosts file on a Debian- or Ubuntu-based system:

```
127.0.0.1 localhost
127.0.1.1 my-new-hostname
```

> **Note** The use of 127.0.1.1 to map the system's hostname is a convention specific to Debian and Ubuntu. Other Linux distributions may instead map the system hostname to the machine's primary IP address (e.g., 192.168.1.10 my-hostname). Always follow your distribution's best practices for hostname mapping.

The structure is simple:

```
<IP address>    <hostname>    [aliases...]
```

If you want to assign custom names to machines in your local network (without using DNS), you can do it here, for example:

```
192.168.1.100    printer.local
```

Now you can ping printer.local from your machine, and it will route to 192.168.1.100.

/etc/resolv.conf: DNS Server Configuration

This file tells your system where to go when it needs to resolve a domain name.

Here's a basic example:

```
nameserver 8.8.8.8
nameserver 8.8.4.4
```

These entries tell the system to use Google's public DNS servers. You can list multiple nameserver entries; your system tries them in order.

> **Note** On many modern Linux systems, /etc/resolv.conf is managed by a network manager (like systemd-resolved, NetworkManager, or Netplan) and may be overwritten at boot or when network settings change. To make persistent DNS changes, consult your system's networking configuration tools.

Editing /etc/resolv.conf

In older Linux systems, you could directly edit /etc/resolv.conf to configure DNS servers. However, on **modern distributions**, this file is often **auto-generated** by tools such as

- systemd-resolved
- resolvconf
- NetworkManager

If you edit /etc/resolv.conf directly and notice your changes are lost after a reboot or network restart, **this is why**. These tools regenerate the file based on dynamic network configuration.

Important Notes

On some distributions or **custom setups**, /etc/resolv.conf **is still managed manually**. Always check your system's configuration before making changes.

CHAPTER 9   NETWORKING AND REMOTE ACCESS

In systems using systemd-resolved, /etc/resolv.conf is often a **symlink** to one of the following:

- /run/systemd/resolve/stub-resolv.conf
- /run/systemd/resolve/resolv.conf

You can check where it points using

```
ls -l /etc/resolv.conf
```

If you want to use a custom DNS setup persistently, you'll need to configure the appropriate tool:

For **systemd-resolved**, use

```
/etc/systemd/resolved.conf
```

Then restart the service with

```
$ sudo systemctl restart systemd-resolved
```

For **NetworkManager**, configure DNS in your connection profile or through a GUI tool.

For systems using **resolvconf**, changes must be made to configuration files that feed into it, such as /etc/network/interfaces or network manager scripts.

For more on systemd-resolved, see the official documentation (https://www.freedesktop.org/software/systemd/man/latest/systemd-resolved.service.html).

systemd-resolved vs. resolvconf

systemd-resolved is part of the systemd suite, and it's becoming the standard way to manage DNS settings on many modern Linux distributions (like Ubuntu).

It manages DNS resolution and integrates with services like DHCP, VPNs, and local DNS caches.

To check if it's running:

```
$ systemctl status systemd-resolved
● systemd-resolved.service - Network Name Resolution
    Loaded: loaded (/usr/lib/systemd/system/systemd-resolved.service;
    enabled; preset: enabled)
    Active: active (running) since Wed 2025-08-13 21:16:50 EAT; 21h ago
```

```
         Docs: man:systemd-resolved.service(8)
               man:org.freedesktop.resolve1(5)
               https://www.freedesktop.org/wiki/Software/systemd/writing-
               network-configuration-managers
               https://www.freedesktop.org/wiki/Software/systemd/writing-
               resolver-clients
     Main PID: 715 (systemd-resolve)
       Status: "Processing requests..."
        Tasks: 1 (limit: 4491)
       Memory: 5.9M (peak: 17.6M swap: 10.6M swap peak: 10.6M)
          CPU: 2.508s
       CGroup: /system.slice/systemd-resolved.service
               └─715 /usr/lib/systemd/systemd-resolved
```

If it's active, it's managing /etc/resolv.conf, but not directly. Instead, /etc/resolv.conf is usually a symlink to /run/systemd/resolve/stub-resolv.conf or another file managed by systemd.

Viewing DNS Configuration with resolvectl

To check your system's current DNS setup when using systemd-resolved, use

```
$ resolvectl status
Global
           Protocols: -LLMNR -mDNS -DNSOverTLS DNSSEC=no/unsupported
    resolv.conf mode: stub
  Current DNS Server: 127.0.0.1
         DNS Servers: 127.0.0.1
Fallback DNS Servers: 8.8.8.8

Link 2 (eno1)
      Current Scopes: none
           Protocols: -DefaultRoute -LLMNR -mDNS -DNSOverTLS DNSSEC=no/
           unsupported

Link 3 (wlp2s0)
      Current Scopes: DNS
```

CHAPTER 9   NETWORKING AND REMOTE ACCESS

```
       Protocols: +DefaultRoute -LLMNR -mDNS -DNSOverTLS DNSSEC=no/
       unsupported
Current DNS Server: 192.168.1.1
       DNS Servers: 192.168.1.1
        DNS Domain: bbrouter
```

What This Means

- The **Global** section shows the system-wide DNS settings.
- The line resolv.conf mode: stub means /etc/resolv.conf points to the **local stub resolver** provided by systemd-resolved.
- That's why you see

    Current DNS Server: 127.0.0.1

    DNS Servers: 127.0.0.1

But **this doesn't mean 127.0.0.1 is your actual upstream DNS server**.

Note   In stub mode, 127.0.0.1 is just the local interface of systemd-resolved. The **real upstream DNS servers** are listed under the corresponding **"Link" section(s)**—like wlp2s0 or eno1—in the DNS Servers: line. These are the servers your system is actually querying.

In the example above, the active interface wlp2s0 shows

   Current DNS Server: 192.168.1.1

   DNS Servers: 192.168.1.1

This indicates the upstream DNS is the router at 192.168.1.1.

For full details, see the systemd-resolved documentation (https://www.freedesktop.org/software/systemd/man/latest/resolved.conf.html).

resolvconf

Another tool that might be in use is resolvconf. It works similarly but is older and less integrated with systemd. It's often used on distributions that don't fully use systemd or with custom network setups.

You configure it by modifying scripts or dropping files into /etc/resolvconf/resolv.conf.d/.

If you're unsure which one your system uses, check if /etc/resolv.conf is a symlink:

```
$ ls -l /etc/resolv.conf
lrwxrwxrwx. 1 root root 39 Apr 24  2024 /etc/resolv.conf -> ../run/systemd/resolve/stub-resolv.conf
```

In that case, systemd-resolved is in charge.

How DNS Lookups Work on Linux

Let's walk through what happens when you type a command like

```
$ ping example.com
```

Here's what Linux does behind the scenes.

Check /etc/hosts

Linux first checks the /etc/hosts file to see if example.com is listed there. If it finds a match, it uses that IP address immediately.

Check nsswitch.conf

The system then consults /etc/nsswitch.conf, which tells it in what order to use name services.

Here's a typical line:

>   hosts: files dns

CHAPTER 9   NETWORKING AND REMOTE ACCESS

This tells the system to

1. Check files (i.e., /etc/hosts).

2. Then query dns (via /etc/resolv.conf).

You can also have other methods like mdns, wins, or ldap depending on your setup.

Use the DNS Server

If the name wasn't found in /etc/hosts, Linux uses the nameservers listed in /etc/resolv.conf. These are usually provided:

- Manually (by you)
- Automatically (via DHCP)
- By VPN software or other network managers

The system sends a DNS query to the first server in the list. If it doesn't respond, it tries the next. The DNS server replies with the corresponding IP address (e.g., 93.184.216.34 for example.com), and the system uses that IP to initiate the connection.

Key Takeaways

- Use hostnamectl to view or set your system's hostname.
- Use /etc/hosts for custom local name resolutions.
- DNS servers are configured in /etc/resolv.conf, but this file is often managed by system services.
- Understand whether your system uses systemd-resolved, resolvconf, or another resolver.
- DNS lookup follows a predictable chain: /etc/hosts → nsswitch.conf → DNS servers.

Static vs. Dynamic IP Addressing

Network interfaces on Linux systems can be assigned IP addresses either dynamically using DHCP (Dynamic Host Configuration Protocol) or statically using manually defined settings.

Dynamic IP Addressing

- Easier to manage
- Automatically assigns IP addresses from a DHCP server
- Useful in environments where devices join and leave frequently (e.g., desktops, laptops)

Static IP Addressing

- Manually assigned IP addresses
- Useful for servers and network devices that require consistent IPs

Note Static IPs are essential for services like web servers, DNS servers, and SSH, where consistency and reliability are key.

Editing Network Configuration Files

Linux distributions handle network interfaces differently. Below are the most common methods used in popular distros.

Debian/Ubuntu

Old Method: /etc/network/interfaces

This was the traditional way to configure network interfaces:

```
$ sudo nano /etc/network/interfaces
```

Example configuration (static IP):

```
auto eth0
iface eth0 inet static
    address 192.168.1.100
    netmask 255.255.255.0
    gateway 192.168.1.1
```

Explanation:

- auto eth0: Enable the interface on boot.
- iface eth0 inet static: Use static IP instead of DHCP.
- address, netmask, gateway: Manual network settings.

Configuring DNS with Netplan (/etc/netplan/*.yaml)

Netplan is the default network configuration tool on **modern Ubuntu systems**, especially **server and cloud images**.

Note Netplan was introduced in Ubuntu 17.10 and became the default on many Ubuntu Server and cloud installations starting with **Ubuntu 18.04 LTS**. It is still used in newer versions like 20.04, 22.04, and 24.04—but availability can depend on the image type (desktop vs. server, minimal vs. full install).

Netplan uses human-readable **YAML** files for configuration, typically located in /etc/netplan/

You can edit the configuration file (e.g., 01-netcfg.yaml) using a text editor:

```
$ sudo nano /etc/netplan/01-netcfg.yaml
```

Add the following lines:

```
network:
  version: 2
  ethernets:
    eth0:
      dhcp4: no
      addresses:
        - 192.168.1.100/24
      gateway4: 192.168.1.1
      nameservers:
        addresses: [8.8.8.8, 8.8.4.4]
```

This configuration

- Disables DHCP for eth0
- Assigns a static IP address
- Sets a default gateway
- Configures Google DNS servers

Apply the Configuration

Once you've saved your changes, apply them with

```
$ sudo netplan apply
```

Tip If there's a syntax error in your YAML, Netplan will fail to apply the config. You can validate the file with sudo netplan try, which gives you a chance to roll back if networking fails.

Red Hat/CentOS/Fedora Networking

Modern Red Hat-based systems (including CentOS Stream and Fedora) primarily use **NetworkManager** for network configuration. Two common methods are

- Using nmcli (recommended for most modern systems)
- Using legacy network scripts (deprecated on newer versions)

Using nmcli (NetworkManager Command-Line Tool)

nmcli is the recommended way to configure networking on

- RHEL 8 and newer
- CentOS 8+, CentOS Stream
- Fedora Workstation/Server

View existing connections:

```
$ nmcli con show
NAME            UUID                                    TYPE      DEVICE
System eth0     12345678-90ab-cdef-1234-567890abcdef    ethernet  eth0
```

Tip If you're unsure of the connection name, first run nmcli device status to see devices and their associated connections.

Configure a static IP with DNS:

```
$ nmcli con mod "System eth0" ipv4.addresses 192.168.1.100/24
$ nmcli con mod "System eth0" ipv4.gateway 192.168.1.1
$ nmcli con mod "System eth0" ipv4.dns "8.8.8.8 8.8.4.4"
$ nmcli con mod "System eth0" ipv4.method manual
```

Tip Without quotes, or with the wrong format, the ipv4.dns line may only apply the first server or cause an error. Use space-separated values in quotes for multiple servers.

Apply the configuration:

```
$ nmcli con up "System eth0"
```

If this fails: The connection name may differ from what you expected. Run nmcli con show to confirm the exact name.

Using Legacy Network Scripts *(Deprecated)*

On older systems or certain minimal installs, you may still encounter network configuration files under

/etc/sysconfig/network-scripts/

Edit the relevant interface file (e.g. ifcfg-eth0):

```
$ sudo nano /etc/sysconfig/network-scripts/ifcfg-eth0
```

Example static configuration:

```
DEVICE=eth0
BOOTPROTO=static
ONBOOT=yes
IPADDR=192.168.1.100
NETMASK=255.255.255.0
GATEWAY=192.168.1.1
DNS1=8.8.8.8
DNS2=8.8.4.4
```

To apply changes:

```
$ sudo systemctl restart network
```

Note This command works **only** if your system is using the legacy network service. On most modern RHEL/Fedora/CentOS systems, networking is managed by **NetworkManager**, and you should use

```
$ sudo systemctl restart NetworkManager
```

Package Management Note

Modern RHEL-based systems (RHEL 8+, CentOS +, Fedora) use

- dnf as the default package manager.
- yum is still available as a **compatibility wrapper**.

When installing networking tools, prefer

```
$ sudo dnf install NetworkManager
```

Troubleshooting Network Interfaces

When diagnosing network issues, these basic commands can help you identify problems with your interface, IP assignment, routing, or DNS.

CHAPTER 9 NETWORKING AND REMOTE ACCESS

Check Interface and IP Address

Use ip a to view all network interfaces and their IP addresses:

```
$ ip a
2: ens33: <BROADCAST,MULTICAST,UP,LOWER_UP> ...
    inet 192.168.1.100/24 brd 192.168.1.255 scope global ens33
```

> **Note** Modern Linux systems often use **predictable network interface names** (like ens33, eno1, enp0s3) instead of the older eth0. Use ip a to identify the correct name on your system.

Test Network Connectivity

Ping the default gateway:

```
$ ping 192.168.1.1

PING 192.168.1.1 (192.168.1.1) 56(84) bytes of data.
64 bytes from 192.168.1.1: icmp_seq=1 ttl=64 time=0.231 ms
Ping an external host: $ ping google.com
PING google.com (142.250.64.78) 56(84) bytes of data.
64 bytes from 142.250.64.78: icmp_seq=1 ttl=115 time=15.2 ms
If the IP ping works but domain names fail, it's likely a DNS issue.

Check Routing Table
$ ip route
default via 192.168.1.1 dev eth0
192.168.1.0/24 dev eth0 proto kernel scope link src 192.168.1.100
```

Restart Interface or NetworkManager

To manually cycle a network interface (replace ens33 with your actual interface name):

```
$ sudo ip link set ens33 down
$ sudo ip link set ens33 up
```

To restart **NetworkManager** (recommended on most Red Hat, Fedora, Ubuntu Desktop systems):

```
$ sudo systemctl restart NetworkManager
```

View Logs from NetworkManager

To inspect recent network activity, use

```
$ journalctl -u NetworkManager -b
Oct 09 14:05:01 hostname NetworkManager[...]: ens33: connected to 192.168.1.100
```

The -b flag limits logs to the **current boot**, making it easier to debug recent changes.

Setting Up SSH for Remote Access

Secure Shell (SSH) allows remote login and command execution. Most Linux systems include OpenSSH tools, but you may need to install and configure the server component.

Installing SSH

Debian/Ubuntu

```
$ sudo apt update
$ sudo apt install openssh-server
```

Red Hat/CentOS/Fedora

```
$ sudo dnf install openssh-server
```

> **Note** On many RHEL-based systems, openssh-server is already installed by default. The systemd service name is sshd, even if the package is called openssh-server.

Enable and start the SSH service:

```
$ sudo systemctl enable sshd
$ sudo systemctl start sshd
```

Check SSH Service Status

To verify the service is running:

```
$ sudo systemctl status sshd
● sshd.service - OpenSSH Daemon
   Loaded: loaded (/usr/lib/systemd/system/sshd.service; enabled)
   Active: active (running) since ...
```

If the service restarts with no errors, systemctl will report **"active (running)"**.

Configure SSH Settings

Edit the SSH server configuration:

```
$ sudo nano /etc/ssh/sshd_config
```

Suggested options:

PermitRootLogin no

PasswordAuthentication no

AllowUsers yourusername

Tip

- Set PasswordAuthentication no when using SSH key–based authentication to reduce brute-force risks.

- PermitRootLogin no disables root login entirely. For older versions of OpenSSH, PermitRootLogin prohibit-password may be used to allow root login **only with keys**.

- Always test access before applying strict settings to avoid being locked out.

CHAPTER 9   NETWORKING AND REMOTE ACCESS

Apply changes:

```
$ sudo systemctl restart sshd
```

Managing SSH Access Through Firewalls

Debian/Ubuntu: UFW (Uncomplicated Firewall)

Check firewall status:

```
$ sudo ufw status
```

Allow SSH:

```
$ sudo ufw allow ssh
```

```
To                         Action      From
--                         ------      ----
OpenSSH                    ALLOW       Anywhere
```

Red Hat/CentOS/Fedora: firewalld (firewall-cmd)

Check firewalld state:

```
$ sudo firewall-cmd --state
```

Allow SSH permanently:

```
$ sudo firewall-cmd --permanent --add-service=ssh
$ sudo firewall-cmd -reload
```

```
success
success
```

> **Note**   ufw and firewall-cmd are not interchangeable:
> - **UFW** is common on **Ubuntu/Debian** systems.
> - **firewall-cmd** (part of firewalld) is the default on **Red Hat**, **CentOS**, and **Fedora**.

SSH Connection and Key Authentication

SSH key-based authentication is a more secure and convenient alternative to password logins. It uses a public/private key pair to log in without entering your password.

Connect via SSH (Password Login)

```
$ ssh user@192.168.1.100
```

Example:

```
user@192.168.1.100's password:
Welcome to Ubuntu ...
```

Set Up SSH Key Authentication

If you haven't already generated an SSH key pair:

```
$ ssh-keygen
```

Then use ssh-copy-id to transfer your public key to the remote system:

```
$ ssh-copy-id user@remote-host
```

Example output:

```
Number of key(s) added: 1
Now try logging into the machine with: "ssh 'user@remote-host'"
```

ssh-copy-id is available on most Linux distributions. **On minimal installations or containers, it may not be installed.**

Manual Alternative to ssh-copy-id

If ssh-copy-id is not available, you can manually copy the public key:
   On your local machine, display the public key:

```
$ cat ~/.ssh/id_rsa.pub
```

   On the remote machine, open (or create) the ~/.ssh/authorized_keys file:

```
$ mkdir -p ~/.ssh
$ nano ~/.ssh/authorized_keys
```

Paste the public key on a new line and save the file.

Set correct permissions:

```
$ chmod 700 ~/.ssh
$ chmod 600 ~/.ssh/authorized_keys
```

Test the Connection

Now you can SSH into the remote system **without a password**:

```
$ ssh user@remote-host
```

Remote Access Logging and Monitoring

When it comes to administering Linux systems, knowing who accessed your server, when, and from where is not optional; it's critical for security, auditing, and troubleshooting. Every SSH login, logout, and failed attempt leaves a footprint. As a system administrator, learning to read these logs and monitor access gives you control and visibility over your system.

In this section, we'll cover

- Accessing log files like /var/log/auth.log and /var/log/secure
- Monitoring live and historical user sessions with w, who, and last
- Using journalctl for SSH service logs
- Tips for proactive monitoring

Understanding Linux Log Files for SSH

Different Linux distributions log authentication events in different files.

- Debian/Ubuntu: /var/log/auth.log
- Red Hat/CentOS/Fedora: /var/log/secure

These files record both successful and failed login attempts, including SSH access.

CHAPTER 9   NETWORKING AND REMOTE ACCESS

View the latest SSH log entries:

```
sudo tail -f /var/log/auth.log
 or on RHEL/CentOS systems
$ sudo tail -f /var/log/secure

Aug 14 08:45:10 server sshd[1745]: Accepted password for user1 from 192.168.1.10 port 51522 ssh2
Aug 14 08:45:12 server sshd[1745]: pam_unix(sshd:session): session opened for user user1 by (uid=0)
Aug 14 09:01:23 server sshd[1745]: pam_unix(sshd:session): session closed for user user1
```

These lines show

- Login accepted for user1
- Source IP: 192.168.1.10
- Session start and end timestamps

To search for all SSH logins by a user:

```
$ sudo grep 'Accepted' /var/log/auth.log | grep 'user1'
```

To find failed attempts:

```
$ sudo grep 'Failed password' /var/log/auth.log
```

Using who, w, and last

These classic commands are great for quick, human-readable insights into user activity.

who: See Currently Logged-In Users

```
$ who
user1    pts/0         2025-08-14 08:45 (192.168.1.10)
```

Shows

- Username
- Terminal (pts/0 = pseudo terminal via SSH)

CHAPTER 9   NETWORKING AND REMOTE ACCESS

- Login time
- Source IP or hostname

w: See Who Is Logged In and What They're Doing

```
$ w
08:55:34 up  2:13,  2 users,  load average: 0.00, 0.01, 0.05
USER     TTY      FROM             LOGIN@   IDLE   JCPU   PCPU WHAT
user1    pts/0    192.168.1.10     08:45    1:00   0.03s  0.03s -bash
```

Breakdown:

- IDLE: How long the user has been idle
- JCPU: Total CPU time for the user's session
- WHAT: Current process the user is running (e.g., bash, top, vim)

last: Show Login History

```
$ last

user1    pts/0        192.168.1.10     Thu Aug 14 08:45    still logged in
user2    pts/1        203.0.113.42     Wed Aug 13 18:02 - 19:45  (01:43)
```

Highlights:

- Users' login and logout times
- IP address of origin
- Duration of session

Viewing SSH Service Logs with journalctl

On systems using systemd (most modern distros), you can get access logs for SSH using

```
$ journalctl
```

View all SSH-related logs:

```
sudo journalctl -u sshd
Aug 14 08:45:10 server sshd[1745]: Accepted password for user1 from
192.168.1.10 port 51522 ssh2
Aug 14 09:01:23 server sshd[1745]: Session closed for user1
```

Filter by date:

```
$ sudo journalctl -u sshd --since "1 hour ago"
```

Use -f to follow logs in real time (like tail -f):

```
$ sudo journalctl -u sshd -f
```

Detecting Failed Login Attempts

Failed logins can signal either a mistyped password or a brute-force attack.

Show failed attempts in /var/log/auth.log:

```
$ sudo grep "Failed password" /var/log/auth.log
Aug 14 10:21:17 server sshd[2083]: Failed password for invalid user admin
from 203.0.113.42 port 55822 ssh2
```

Find repeated attempts (possible brute-force):

```
$ sudo grep "Failed password" /var/log/auth.log | awk '{print (NF-3)}' |
sort | uniq -c | sort -nr | head
15 203.0.113.42
12 192.0.2.15
```

This shows the number of failed attempts per IP.

Tip   Use fail2ban to block brute-force IPs automatically.

Install on Debian/Ubuntu:

```
$ sudo apt install fail2ban
```

Start and enable:

```
$ sudo systemctl enable --now fail2ban
```

Proactive Monitoring Tools

Beyond logs, you can use tools or simple scripts to monitor remote access in real time.

Tracking Logins with the Linux Audit Daemon (auditd)

The **Linux Audit Daemon** (auditd) provides detailed logging of security-relevant events including **user logins**, **authentication failures**, **privilege escalation**, and **file access**.

Install and Start auditd

Ubuntu/Debian

```
$ sudo apt update
$ sudo apt install auditd
$ sudo systemctl start auditd
```

Red Hat/CentOS/Fedora

```
$ sudo dnf install audit
$ sudo systemctl enable --now auditd
```

View Login Events

To view login-related events:

```
$ sudo ausearch -m USER_LOGIN
```

This shows records for both successful and failed login attempts, including the username, terminal, timestamp, and more.

CHAPTER 9 NETWORKING AND REMOTE ACCESS

Note on Configuration

auditd **won't track everything by default**—it requires configuration to define **what to monitor**.

- Some login tracking is available out of the box, but for full auditing (e.g., tracking file access, command execution, or sudo usage), you'll need to define **audit rules**.

- Use auditctl to set temporary rules:

    ```
    $ sudo auditctl -l
    $ sudo auditctl -a always,exit -F arch=b64 -S execve
    ```

    For persistent rules, use

    /etc/audit/rules.d/

    See the official auditd documentation for rule syntax and advanced usage.

Remote Desktop and GUI Access

While the command line is king in Linux system administration, there are times when you need a Graphical user interface (GUI). Maybe you're managing a remote desktop system, running GUI apps, or supporting users who aren't comfortable with the terminal. In such cases, remote desktop and GUI access tools become essential.

This section covers

- When and why GUI access is useful
- Tools like VNC, xRDP, and Remmina
- Running individual GUI apps remotely with ssh -X or ssh -Y
- Security and performance tips

When Do You Need Remote GUI Access?

Not all tasks require a GUI, but here are a few valid use cases:

- Supporting users on remote desktop environments
- Running GUI applications (like Gedit, Firefox, or GIMP) remotely

CHAPTER 9 NETWORKING AND REMOTE ACCESS

- Managing desktop environments on headless servers (rare, but possible)
- Administrating systems where GUI tools are the norm (e.g., Ubuntu Desktop, Linux Mint)

Option 1: Using VNC (Virtual Network Computing)

VNC allows you to remotely control a Linux desktop environment from another computer over the network. It works by transmitting keyboard and mouse events from the client to the server and relaying screen updates back in the other direction. It's especially useful for persistent sessions where you want to leave a desktop running on a remote machine and return to it later.

Setting Up a VNC Server on the Remote Host

If you already have a **desktop environment** installed (e.g., GNOME, common on Ubuntu, CentOS, RHEL), you can skip installing a new desktop environment and just set up the VNC server.

Ubuntu/Debian-based:

```
$ sudo apt update
$ sudo apt install tightvncserver
```

RHEL/CentOS:

```
$ sudo dnf install tigervnc-server
```

Start the VNC server and set a password:

```
$ vncserver
```

You'll be prompted to set a password for VNC access. This also creates the ~/.vnc directory and a default startup file.

Configure VNC to use GNOME:
Edit the VNC startup script:

```
$ nano ~/.vnc/xstart
```

CHAPTER 9 NETWORKING AND REMOTE ACCESS

Add the following contents:

```
#!/bin/sh
exec gnome-session &
```

On some systems, you may need to use exec /usr/bin/gnome-session & depending on where GNOME is installed.

Make it executable:

```
$ chmod +x ~/.vnc/xstartup
```

Restart the VNC server:

```
$ vncserver -kill :1
$ vncserver :1
```

This starts the VNC session on display :1 (which maps to TCP port 5901).

Connect from a client (e.g., Remmina or RealVNC Viewer):

On your local machine:

- Open Remmina (Linux) or RealVNC Viewer (Windows/macOS).
- Connect to remote_ip:5901.
- Enter your VNC password.

Note   VNC does **not encrypt** traffic by default. It's strongly recommended to tunnel your VNC connection over SSH.

Secure VNC with SSH Tunneling

To prevent your VNC session from being exposed in plaintext over the network:

On your **local machine**, create an SSH tunnel:

```
ssh -L 5901:localhost:5901 user@remote_ip
```

Then, in your VNC client, connect to

```
localhost:5901
```

This way, all VNC traffic is routed securely through SSH.

Using xRDP (Windows-Compatible Remote Desktop)

xRDP allows you to connect to a Linux desktop using the built-in Remote Desktop Connection app in Windows. It's easy for mixed environments.

Install xRDP on Linux

```
$ sudo apt install xrdp
```

Start and enable the service:

```
$ sudo systemctl enable xrdp
$ sudo systemctl start xrdp
```

Check status:

```
$ sudo systemctl status xrdp

xrdp.service - xrdp daemon
   Active: active (running)
```

Make sure a desktop environment is installed (like XFCE, GNOME, or MATE). On Ubuntu Server, install a desktop first:

```
$ sudo apt install xfce4
```

Edit xRDP session config (optional):

```
echo "startxfce4" > ~/.xsession
```

Connect from Windows or Remmina

- Open Remote Desktop Connection (search mstsc.exe).
- Enter the IP address of the Linux system.
- Log in with your Linux user credentials.

That's it, you'll have full remote desktop access!

Running GUI Apps over SSH (SSH Tunneling)

Want to open a single GUI application (like Gedit or Firefox) without launching a full remote desktop environment? You can use **X11 forwarding over SSH**, which streams the app window to your local machine while executing it remotely.

Best suited for: Low-latency networks and lightweight GUI apps

Requirements

- A local X server:
    - Linux: Typically pre-installed.
    - Windows: Use VcXsrv or Xming.
    - macOS: Use XQuartz.
- The remote server must have X11 forwarding enabled in SSH.

Server Side: Enable X11 Forwarding in SSH

Edit the SSH daemon configuration:

```
$ sudo nano /etc/ssh/sshd_config
```

Ensure the following lines are present and **not commented out**:

X11Forwarding yes

X11DisplayOffset 10

Then restart the SSH service:

```
$ sudo systemctl restart sshd
```

Client Side: Connect with X11 Forwarding

On Linux or macOS:

```
ssh -X user@remote-ip      # Standard forwarding
ssh -Y user@remote-ip      # Trusted forwarding (less secure, but faster)
```

Then run a GUI app remotely:

```
gedit
```

The app window will appear on your local desktop but run on the remote server.

Important: X11 Forwarding and Wayland Limitations

Modern Linux distributions (e.g., Ubuntu 22.04+, Fedora, GNOME 40+) often use **Wayland** instead of the traditional **X11 display server**. This can **break or limit X11 forwarding**.

Common Issues Under Wayland

- GUI apps may fail to launch over SSH.
- You'll get errors like you cannot open display or no window appears.
- Clipboard or input redirection might not work correctly.

Workarounds and Solutions

1. **Use XWayland** (automatic fallback for some apps):

   a. Most desktop environments still support X11 apps via **XWayland**, a compatibility layer.

   b. If available, apps may launch, but behavior can be inconsistent.

2. **Switch to an X11 session temporarily:**

   a. On the login screen, select an "X11" session (e.g., GNOME on X11) instead of Wayland.

   b. This restores full X11 forwarding functionality.

3. **Use VNC or xRDP instead of X11 forwarding:**

   a. For persistent or complex remote GUI sessions, consider using a full remote desktop solution.

CHAPTER 9   NETWORKING AND REMOTE ACCESS

Tips for Windows users:

- Use **PuTTY** with X11 forwarding enabled:
- In PuTTY, go to

    Connection ➤ SSH ➤ X11

    Then check "Enable X11 forwarding."

- Start **VcXsrv** or **Xming** on your machine **before** connecting.
- Then connect via SSH and run your desired GUI app.

Security and Performance Tips

- Never expose VNC or RDP ports to the public internet. Use an SSH tunnel instead.
- GUI tools use more bandwidth; avoid on slow connections or over mobile hotspots.
- Use fail2ban to protect RDP/VNC ports if you must expose them.
- Test SSH X11 apps with lightweight programs first (xeyes, xclock, etc.)
- Consider Wayland compatibility; some apps don't work with X11 forwarding under Wayland. Use X11 session if needed.

Virtual Private Networks (VPNs) and Remote Connections

A Virtual Private Network (VPN) creates a secure, encrypted connection over the internet, allowing users to connect to remote networks safely. VPNs are commonly used for

- Secure remote work access
- Bypassing regional restrictions
- Protecting privacy on public Wi-Fi

CHAPTER 9   NETWORKING AND REMOTE ACCESS

This guide walks you through

- Buying a VPN subscription
- Downloading configuration files
- Setting up OpenVPN or WireGuard
- Testing and using your VPN securely

Let's begin.

Choose and Purchase a VPN Provider

Recommended Linux-friendly VPNs:

- Mullvad: No account required, excellent WireGuard support
- Proton VPN: Secure, open source, supports both protocols
- NordVPN: Popular, fast, works with OpenVPN and WireGuard
- IVPN, PIA, OVPN, etc.

Create an account (except Mullvad, which uses an account number), choose a plan, and pay.

Log In and Download Config Files

Once logged into your VPN provider's website:

For OpenVPN:

- Go to the Downloads or Manual Setup section.
- Download .ovpn files for the locations you want to connect to.
- Some providers let you bundle multiple files in a ZIP and extract them.

For WireGuard:

- Use a configuration generator (like Mullvad or Proton VPN).
- Enter your desired location and settings.
- Download the resulting .conf file (e.g., mullvad-wg.conf).

Setting Up OpenVPN (Client)

OpenVPN allows secure tunneling of your network traffic to a remote VPN server. It uses .ovpn configuration files to manage connection settings and supports both manual and system-managed operation.

Install OpenVPN

On Debian/Ubuntu

```
$ sudo apt update
$
$ sudo apt install openvpn
```

On RHEL/CentOS/Fedora

```
$ sudo dnf install openvpn
```

You may need EPEL enabled on older RHEL-based systems.

Test the VPN Manually

Use the .ovpn file provided by your VPN service to test connectivity:

```
$ sudo openvpn --config ~/Downloads/myvpnfile.ovpn
```

If successful, you should see the following at the end of the output:

```
Initialization Sequence Completed
```

> **Note** This will block the terminal until you stop it with Ctrl + C. It's meant for testing only—not for long-term use.

Store and Configure OpenVPN for systemd

Move your config file into OpenVPN's expected location:

```
$ sudo cp ~/Downloads/myvpnfile.ovpn /etc/openvpn/client/
```

Then rename it to .conf so it can be managed by systemd:

```
$ sudo mv /etc/openvpn/client/myvpnfile.ovpn /etc/openvpn/client/myvpnfile.conf
```

Next, ensure the file is owned by root and not world-readable:

```
$ sudo chown root:root /etc/openvpn/client/myvpnfile.conf
```

```
$ sudo chmod 600 /etc/openvpn/client/myvpnfile.conf
```

Add Login Credentials (Optional)

If your .ovpn file requires a **username and password**, create a separate credentials file:

```
$ sudo nano /etc/openvpn/client/auth.txt
```

Add two lines:

```
yourusername
yourpassword
```

Then modify the .conf file to include

```
auth-user-pass /etc/openvpn/client/auth.txt
```

Also restrict access to this credentials file:

```
$ sudo chmod 600 /etc/openvpn/client/auth.txt
```

Start and Enable the OpenVPN Service

Start the VPN connection:

```
$ sudo systemctl start openvpn-client@myvpnfile
```

If this fails, check logs via journalctl -xeu openvpn-client@myvpnfile.
Enable it to run at boot:

```
$ sudo systemctl enable openvpn-client@myvpnfile
```

Check the connection status:

```
$ systemctl status openvpn-client@myvpnfile
```

Systemd Service Name May Vary

The service name format (openvpn-client@myvpnfile) is typical on **Debian/Ubuntu**, but **this varies by distro**, for example:

- Debian/Ubuntu: openvpn-client@myvpnfile.service
- CentOS/RHEL/Fedora: Often openvpn@client.service or openvpn@myvpnfile.service

To list available OpenVPN units on your system:

```
$ systemctl list-units '*openvpn*'
```

Use the exact unit name returned by that command.

Setting Up WireGuard on Ubuntu

WireGuard is a modern VPN protocol praised for its **speed**, **simplicity**, and **strong encryption**. It's often used with provider-generated configuration files (e.g., from Mullvad, Proton VPN), but can also be manually configured.

Option 1: Using a Provider-Generated WireGuard Config

Install WireGuard

```
$ sudo apt update
$ sudo apt install wireguard
```

This installs both wg (for low-level control) and wg-quick (for simple up/down management).

Place the Config File

Move your downloaded WireGuard configuration file to the system directory:

```
$ sudo cp ~/Downloads/mullvad-wg.conf /etc/wireguard/wg0.conf
```

wg-quick looks for /etc/wireguard/wg0.conf by default—rename your config to wg0.conf to make things easier.

Secure the Config File

```
$ sudo chmod 600 /etc/wireguard/wg0.conf
```

This is **very important** because your private key is inside the config file. Improper permissions can expose sensitive data.

Start the VPN

```
$ sudo wg-quick up wg0
```

To disconnect:

```
$ sudo wg-quick down wg0
```

Enable WireGuard at Boot

```
$ sudo systemctl enable wg-quick@wg0
```

Check VPN Status

```
$ sudo wg

interface: wg0
  public key: ABC123...
  private key: (hidden)
  listening port: 51820

peer: XYZ456...
  endpoint: your-vpn-server.com:51820
  allowed ips: 0.0.0.0/0
  latest handshake: 2 minutes ago
  transfer: 1.45 MiB received, 2.15 MiB sent
```

Important Notes

- Private key warning: Never share your private key. If you're generating keys manually (e.g., using wg genkey), protect them:

    chmod 600 privatekey

CHAPTER 9   NETWORKING AND REMOTE ACCESS

- **AllowedIPs = 0.0.0.0/0** means **all your traffic is routed through the VPN**, including DNS and internet access. This is **full-tunnel mode**.
- If you want to use **split tunneling** (only route certain networks through the VPN), adjust your config like this:

    AllowedIPs = 10.0.0.0/24

This will send only traffic for 10.0.0.0/24 through the VPN and the rest through your normal connection.

Option 2: Manual Setup with Your Own Keys

If you're running your own WireGuard server or configuring a custom peer.

Generate Key Pair

```
$ wg genkey | tee privatekey | wg pubkey > publickey
```

- privatekey: Your private key (keep secret).
- publickey: Send this to the server administrator.

Create the WireGuard Config

```
$ sudo nano /etc/wireguard/wg0.conf
```

Paste and edit:

```
[Interface]
PrivateKey = <your-private-key>
Address = 10.0.0.2/24
ListenPort = 51820

[Peer]
PublicKey = <server-public-key>
Endpoint = your-vpn-server.com:51820
AllowedIPs = 0.0.0.0/0
PersistentKeepalive = 25
```

CHAPTER 9   NETWORKING AND REMOTE ACCESS

Explanation:

- PrivateKey: From the key you generated
- Address: Your internal VPN IP (from server or your own plan)
- AllowedIPs = 0.0.0.0/0: Sends all your traffic through the VPN
- PersistentKeepalive = 25: Keeps connection alive behind NAT

Then, run

```
$ sudo chmod 600 /etc/wireguard/wg0.conf
```

And follow the same steps:

```
$ sudo wg-quick up wg0
$ sudo systemctl enable wg-quick@wg0
$ sudo wg
```

Troubleshooting Tips

- DNS leaks: Use a tool like dnsleaktest.com to verify.
- Kill switch: Consider using firewall rules (iptables/ufw) to block internet if VPN disconnects.
- Log errors:
  - OpenVPN: /var/log/syslog or journalctl -u openvpn-client@yourvpn
  - WireGuard: journalctl -u wg-quick@wg0

Secure Remote File Transfer Using SCP and SFTP

Both **SCP** and **SFTP** use **SSH** for encrypted data transfer between systems. However, it's important to note that **scp is considered deprecated in some projects** due to historical issues with remote shell expansion. While it's still widely used, alternatives like sftp or rsync -e ssh are often recommended for better reliability and security.

SCP (Secure Copy)

Copy a file to a remote server:

```
$ scp file.txt user@192.168.1.100:/home/user/
```

Copy a directory recursively:

```
$ scp -r myfolder/ user@192.168.1.100:/home/user/
```

Copy a file from a remote server to local:

```
$ scp user@192.168.1.100:/home/user/file.txt ./
```

Use a non-standard SSH port (e.g., 2222):

```
$ scp -P 2222 file.txt user@192.168.1.100:/home/user/
```

Note Consider using rsync -e ssh for more robust and efficient file synchronization, especially when dealing with large directories or repeat transfers.

SFTP (SSH File Transfer Protocol)

Start an SFTP session:

```
$ sftp user@192.168.1.100
```

Basic SFTP commands:

- ls: List remote files.
- get file.txt: Download a file.
- put file.txt: Upload a file.
- exit: Close the session.

Tips for Secure File Transfer

- **Avoid root logins.** Use regular users with sudo privileges.

- **Use SSH key-based authentication** instead of passwords for automation and improved security.

- **Secure your .ssh directory and files:**

  ```
  chmod 700 ~/.ssh
  chmod 600 ~/.ssh/authorized_keys
  ```

Conclusion

Networking and remote access are cornerstones of Linux system administration. Whether you're configuring static IPs, troubleshooting connectivity, or setting up secure VPNs and file transfers, a deep understanding of these tools will empower you to manage any Linux environment with confidence.

As we continue building a resilient and efficient Linux system, the next critical area to explore is backup and disaster recovery. In Chapter 10, we'll delve into essential backup strategies, explore automation techniques using tools like cron, and outline practical approaches to disaster recovery. From using tools like rsync and tar to planning for system failures and restoring lost data, this chapter will equip you with the knowledge to safeguard your systems against data loss and unexpected disruptions.

CHAPTER 10

Backup and Disaster Recovery

In any system administration environment, especially when dealing with Linux, ensuring the safety and recoverability of data is critical. Data loss can result from hardware failure, accidental deletion, malicious attacks, or even natural disasters. In this chapter, we'll cover strategies and tools for backing up data, automating the backup process, and preparing for disaster recovery.

Backup Strategies

The Importance of Regular Backups

Regular backups are the cornerstone of data security. Without proper backups, the loss of important data due to hardware failure, human error, or malicious attacks can be catastrophic. Here are the reasons why regular backups are indispensable:

- Data loss prevention: Backups protect you from losing critical files, configurations, or even entire systems.

- Business continuity: Regular backups ensure that your systems can be quickly restored, minimizing downtime.

- Compliance and legal requirements: In many industries, regular backups are a legal requirement for business continuity.

CHAPTER 10   BACKUP AND DISASTER RECOVERY

For best practices:

- Back up frequently: Daily or weekly, depending on the importance of the data.
- Store backups offsite: This prevents data loss in case of physical damage to the primary site.
- Test recovery periodically: Backup files are only useful if you can restore them.

Before You Start Backing Up, Follow This Checklist

- Use **absolute paths** in all backup/restore commands.
- Run as **non-root** unless needed (e.g., for dd).
- Confirm device names with lsblk before using dd.
- Use --dry-run or preview modes before any actual sync.
- Keep **at least one copy** of important data in a separate location.
- Validate your backups after creating them (see the "How to Test and Validate Your Backups" section).

Backup Tools: rsync, tar, and Others

Linux provides various powerful tools to facilitate backups. Here are some of the most used.

rsync: Remote Sync

rsync is one of the most used and efficient backup tools in Linux. It's a fast and flexible tool that can be used for both local and remote backups. It's especially powerful because it uses a method called **delta encoding**, meaning only the changes (deltas) in files are copied during subsequent backups, making it ideal for incremental backups.

How Does rsync Work?

rsync compares files between the source and destination and only transfers the data that has been modified. This makes it much faster than copying everything over again, and it saves bandwidth if you're using it for remote backups. Additionally, it can preserve file permissions, ownership, timestamps, and symbolic links.

Common use cases for rsync:

- Local backups: Copy files from one directory to another on the same machine.
- Remote backups: Transfer files between systems over SSH.
- Incremental backups: Create backups that only include the changes made since the last backup.

Basic rsync syntax:

```
rsync [OPTIONS] SOURCE DEST
```

- SOURCE: The source file or directory
- DEST: The destination file or directory
- OPTIONS: Flags that modify the behavior of rsync

Basic Example: Local Backup

Let's say we want to back up a directory (/home/user/data/) to a backup location (/backup/data/). Here is how we'll go about it:

```
$ rsync -av /home/user/data/ /backup/data/
```

- -a: Archive mode, which preserves symbolic links, permissions, timestamps, etc.
- -v: Verbose mode, which provides detailed output about what's being copied.
- --delete: Optionally, you can use this flag to delete files in the destination directory that no longer exist in the source directory.

Example with Remote Backup

You can also use rsync to back up data to a remote server via SSH. This is especially useful for offsite backups.

```
$ rsync -avz /home/user/data/ user@remote_host:/backup/data/
```

- -z: Enables compression, which is useful for reducing data transfer size over a network.
- user@remote_host: Replace this with your username and the IP or domain of the remote server.

Example of Incremental Backup with rsync

When creating backups, you typically want to back up only new or modified files. The rsync tool provides an efficient way to do this using the --link-dest option, which enables incremental backups by creating **hard links** to unchanged files from a previous backup, instead of copying them again. This saves disk space and reduces backup time.

Important Notes About --link-dest

- The --link-dest path must be **relative to the destination directory**, not the source.
- The destination directory (where the backup is being stored) **must be on a POSIX-compliant filesystem that supports hard links** (e.g., ext4, XFS). If the destination and the --link-dest target are on different filesystems, **hard linking will fail**, and rsync will copy all files instead.
- The --link-dest option should point to a **previous full or incremental backup**.

Example Directory Layout

Assume the following directory structure:

```
/backups/
├── 2023-10-01/        # Full backup
├── 2023-10-02/        # Incremental backup (links to 2023-10-01)
└── 2023-10-03/        # Next incremental (links to 2023-10-02)
```

Example Command

To create an incremental backup on 2023-10-02 that links to the previous backup (2023-10-01), run

```
$ rsync -av --link-dest=../2023-10-01 /source/directory/ /backups/2023-10-02/
```

This command

- Copies new and modified files from /source/directory/ into /backups/2023-10-02/
- Creates hard links for all unchanged files from /backups/2023-10-01/

Note Ensure that /backups/2023-10-01/ and /backups/2023-10-02/ reside on the same filesystem so that hard links can be created.

Tips **Include a trailing slash / on the source directory** when using rsync. This ensures that **only the contents** of the directory are copied, **not the directory itself**.

```
$ rsync -av /home/user/data/ /backup/data/
```

In this example:

- Files *inside* /home/user/data/ will be copied directly into /backup/data/.
- If you omit the trailing /, the entire data directory will be copied into /backup/data/data/, which may not be what you want.

Use --dry-run to preview the operation before running it for real. This shows what would be copied, deleted, or updated, without making any actual changes:

```
$ rsync -av --dry-run /home/user/data/ /backup/data/
```

This is especially useful when using --delete, --link-dest, or scripting backups, to avoid surprises.

tar

tar is one of the oldest and most widely used Linux backup tools. It is often used to bundle a collection of files and directories into a single archive file, which can then be compressed. While it's traditionally used for creating archives, it is also effective for backup purposes.

How Does tar Work?

The tar command creates an archive of the specified files or directories and, optionally, compresses the archive. It's particularly useful when you need to back up entire directories or systems, as it's capable of preserving file permissions, ownership, and timestamps.

Common use cases for tar:

- Full backups: Create a backup of an entire directory or system.
- Compressed backups: Bundle and compress files to save space.
- Portable backups: Create a single archive that's easy to move or store.

Basic tar syntax:

```
tar [OPTIONS] -f ARCHIVE_NAME FILES_TO_BACKUP
```

- ARCHIVE_NAME: The name of the backup archive file
- FILES_TO_BACKUP: The files or directories you want to include in the backup
- OPTIONS: Flags that modify the behavior of tar

Basic Example: Creating a Compressed Backup

In this example, we want to back up the /home/user/data/ directory to a compressed archive (backup.tar.gz):

```
$ tar -czvf backup.tar.gz /home/user/data/
```

Explanation:

- -c: Create a new archive.
- -z: Compress the archive using gzip.
- -v: Verbose mode, which lists the files being added.
- -f: Specifies the name of the archive file.

This command will create a backup.tar.gz file containing the contents of /home/user/data/.

Example of Extracting Files from a Backup

To restore the files from a tar archive, you can use the -x flag to extract the archive:

```
$ tar -xzvf backup.tar.gz -C /restore/directory
```

Explanation:

- -x: Extract the archive.
- -C: Specifies the directory to which the files should be extracted.

Example of Incremental Backup with tar

tar can also be used for incremental backups using the --listed-incremental option. This creates a snapshot of the current filesystem and only backs up files that have changed since the last backup.

```
$ tar --listed-incremental=/path/to/snapshot.file -czvf backup.tar.gz /home/user/data/
```

Explanation:

- --listed-incremental: This option creates an incremental backup using the specified snapshot file.

Tips Use the -p option if you want to preserve the file permissions during extraction.

Always check the integrity of your backups using tar -tvf (to list the contents) before relying on them.

dd: Disk Duplicate

dd is a powerful and low-level tool that is often used for creating disk images or backups of entire drives and partitions. Unlike rsync and tar, which back up files and directories, dd copies data block by block from one device to another. This makes it ideal for creating full disk backups or cloning entire systems.

How Does dd Work?

dd works by copying data from one location to another, byte by byte, making an exact copy. This is useful for backing up partitions, drives, or creating bootable images. It's not ideal for file-level backups, but it is indispensable for full system backups or restoring a disk from an image.

Common use cases for dd:

- Full disk backups: Create a complete image of a disk or partition.
- System cloning: Clone an entire disk to a backup drive or for migration.
- Recovering damaged disks: Create disk images from failing drives for data recovery.

Basic dd syntax:

```
dd if=SOURCE of=DESTINATION [OPTIONS]
```

- if=SOURCE: Input file (source device or file)
- of=DESTINATION: Output file (destination device or file)
- OPTIONS: Flags to control how dd behaves

Basic Example: Creating a Disk Image

Let's say we want to create a backup of the /dev/sda disk and save it as backup.img:

```
$ dd if=/dev/sda of=/path/to/backup.img bs=64K conv=noerror,sync
```

Explanation:

- if=/dev/sda: The input file (the source disk)
- of=/path/to/backup.img: The output file (the backup image)
- bs=64K: Specifies the block size
- conv=noerror,sync: Tells dd to continue on read errors and synchronize the input and output

Restoring from a dd Backup

You can restore a full disk image using the dd command by reversing the original backup operation, reading from the image file and writing directly to a block device.

Note **This process will overwrite all data on the target disk.** Triple-check that you are writing to the correct device. Mistakes (e.g., writing to your system drive) can result in **irreversible data loss**.

Step 1: Identify the Correct Target Device

Before running dd, use the following command to list your available disks safely:

```
$ lsblk -o NAME,SIZE,MOUNTPOINT
```

This will show device names (e.g., sda, sdb) along with their sizes and mount points, so you can identify the correct target. **Make sure the target is not mounted.**

Step 2: Restore the Image

```
sudo dd if=/path/to/backup.img of=/dev/sdX bs=64K conv=noerror,sync status=progress
```

Explanation:

- Replace /dev/sdX with your actual target device (e.g., /dev/sdb), based on the lsblk output.
- bs=64K improves performance by increasing block size.

- conv=noerror,sync tells dd to continue on read errors and pad missing data.
- status=progress (GNU dd only) shows a live progress bar.

Checking for status=progress Support

You can check whether your system's dd supports status=progress by running

```
$ dd --help | grep status
```

If unsupported, you can use pv (Pipe Viewer) as an alternative:

```
$ sudo pv /path/to/backup.img | sudo dd of=/dev/sdX bs=64K conv=noerror,sync
```

Tips

- Be careful: dd can overwrite data on the target disk, so always double-check your source and destination paths.
- status=progress: This option provides progress information during the backup process.
- Always test the restore process on a **non-critical disk** or virtual machine before performing it on production hardware.

Cloud Backup Options

While traditional backup tools are great for local and remote backups, cloud backups provide an additional layer of protection. Cloud storage solutions offer off-site storage, redundancy, and scalability that local backups cannot match. Here's how you can set up backups to popular cloud storage providers from Linux.

Amazon S3

Amazon S3 (Simple Storage Service) is a highly scalable, durable, and secure object storage service provided by AWS (Amazon Web Services). It allows you to store virtually unlimited amounts of data, from personal backups to enterprise-level storage solutions.

Why Use S3 for Backups?

- Durability: S3 provides 99.999999999% durability (11 nines).
- Scalability: Automatically scales with the amount of data.
- Security: Offers encryption, access controls, and audit logging.

Install the AWS CLI on Linux

Prerequisites:

- A Linux machine (Ubuntu/Debian/CentOS or similar)
- An AWS account
- An S3 bucket (we'll create one if needed)
- IAM user with programmatic access and appropriate permissions

The AWS CLI is a command-line tool that lets you interact with AWS services, including S3.

About AWS CLI Versions

Many Linux distributions include **AWS CLI v1** in their package managers (e.g., apt, dnf).
However, newer features and better compatibility are available in **AWS CLI v2**.
The output shown later in this guide (e.g., aws-cli/2.15.32) assumes **v2**.
To avoid confusion or missing features, it's recommended to install AWS CLI **v2** using the **official method** below.

Method 1: Recommended—Official AWS CLI v2 Installer

Download and install AWS CLI v2:

```
$ curl "https://awscli.amazonaws.com/awscli-exe-linux-x86_64.zip" -o "awscliv2.zip"
$ unzip awscliv2.zip
$ sudo ./aws/install
```

CHAPTER 10 BACKUP AND DISASTER RECOVERY

Verify installation:

```
$ aws --version
aws-cli/2.15.32 Python/3.11.6 Linux/x86_64
```

See full instructions on the official AWS documentation.

Method 2: Optional—Install via the OS Package Manager (May Install v1)

On Ubuntu/Debian:

```
$ sudo apt update
$ sudo apt install awscli -y
```

On **RHEL/CentOS:**

```
$ sudo dnf install awscli -y
```

This may install AWS CLI **v1**, which has limited features and different syntax for some commands.

Check your version with

```
$ aws --version
```

If you see something like aws-cli/1.22.23, consider removing it and switching to the official v2 install method:

```
$ sudo apt remove awscli
```

Tip Always use the latest version of the AWS CLI to access the latest features and bug fixes.

Configure AWS CLI

Run

```
$ aws configure
```

You'll be prompted to enter

```
AWS Access Key ID [None]: AKIAIOSFODNN7EXAMPLE
AWS Secret Access Key [None]: wJalrXUtnFEMI/K7MDENG/bPxRfiCYEXAMPLEKEY
Default region name [None]: us-east-1
Default output format [None]: json
```

Where to Get These?

- Go to the **AWS IAM Console**.
- Create or select a user.
- Assign programmatic access.
- Attach the policy AmazonS3FullAccess (for testing; use least privilege in production).
- Save the Access Key and Secret Key.

Note Never expose or share your Access Key/Secret Key publicly. Store them securely (e.g., in environment variables or AWS credentials files).

Create an S3 Bucket

You can skip this step if you already have an S3 bucket set up for backups.

To create a new bucket from the AWS CLI:

```
$ aws s3 mb s3://my-linux-backup-bucket
```

Replace my-linux-backup-bucket with your desired bucket name.

S3 bucket names must be globally unique—no two AWS accounts can share the same bucket name.

Specify a Region (Recommended)

By default, the bucket will be created in your configured default region.

To explicitly set the region (e.g., US West):

```
$ aws s3 mb s3://my-linux-backup-bucket --region us-west-2
```

Bucket Naming Rules (Strict)

Amazon S3 bucket names must follow specific rules:

- Must be **between 3 and 63 characters**.
- Only lowercase letters, numbers, and hyphens (-).
- **No underscores (_).**
- **No uppercase letters.**
- Must start and end with a **letter or number**.
- Cannot be formatted like an IP address (e.g., 192.168.1.1).
- Must be **globally unique** across all AWS accounts.

In legacy regions (like us-east-1), there may be additional constraints—always test with --region specified if you're unsure.

Tip Use hyphens, not underscores, in bucket names. Avoid uppercase letters.

Prepare the Data to Back Up

Let's say we want to back up the /home/user/data/ directory.

Check the size of the data:

```
$ du -sh /home/user/data
```

Optional: Compress Your Data

```
$ tar -czvf data-backup-$(date +%F).tar.gz /home/user/data
```

This creates a timestamped backup file, such as data-backup-2025-08-16.tar.gz.

Upload Data to S3

You can upload your backup files to Amazon S3 using either aws s3 cp (for individual files) or aws s3 sync (for entire directories).

Option 1: Upload a Single File

```
$ aws s3 cp data-backup-2025-08-16.tar.gz s3://my-linux-backup-bucket/backups/
```

This uploads a single file into the backups/ folder of your S3 bucket.

Option 2: Sync a Directory

```
$ aws s3 sync /home/user/data/ s3://my-linux-backup-bucket/data/ --storage-class STANDARD_IA
```

This command uploads all files in /home/user/data/ to your S3 bucket.

- sync only uploads **new or modified files**.
- --storage-class STANDARD_IA saves cost by storing files in the **Infrequent Access** tier (ideal for backups).

Important Notes About aws s3 sync

--delete (Use with Caution)

- **By default**, aws s3 sync **does not delete files** in the destination bucket that are no longer present locally.
- If you add --delete, it will **remove files from S3** that don't exist in your local directory.

Example (potentially destructive):

```
$ aws s3 sync /home/user/data/ s3://my-linux-backup-bucket/data/ --delete
```

Use --delete carefully—it permanently deletes files from S3 if they're missing locally.

--exact-timestamps Behavior

- The --exact-timestamps flag ensures that files with **identical size but different modification times** are re-uploaded.
- Note: Behavior of --exact-timestamps may differ across AWS CLI versions:
  - In **v1**, it had no effect.
  - In **v2**, it works as expected and is often **enabled by default**.

To force timestamp checking explicitly:

```
$ aws s3 sync /local/path s3://bucket/path --exact-timestamps
```

Best Practices

- Run with --dryrun first to preview what will be uploaded or deleted:

  ```
  $ aws s3 sync /home/user/data/ s3://my-linux-backup-bucket/data/ --dryrun
  ```

- Consider enabling **versioning** on your bucket to protect against accidental deletion or overwrites.

Note sync ensures local and remote directories are mirror images. Deleted local files won't be removed remotely by default; use --delete cautiously.

Automate with cron (Optional but Recommended)

To schedule regular backups (e.g., daily at 2 AM):

```
Edit Crontab
$ crontab -e
Add a Cron Job
0 2 * * * /usr/bin/aws s3 sync /home/user/data/ s3://my-linux-backup-bucket/data/ --storage-class STANDARD_IA >> /var/log/s3_backup.log 2>&1
0 2 * * * → every day at 2:00 AM
Logs are saved to /var/log/s3_backup.log.
```

> **Tip** Make sure no sensitive data (e.g., keys) is hardcoded in cron jobs.

Restore Files from S3

To download a specific file:

`$ aws s3 cp s3://my-linux-backup-bucket/backups/data-backup-2025-08-16.tar.gz .`

To restore an entire folder:

`$ aws s3 sync s3://my-linux-backup-bucket/data/ /home/user/data_restored/`

Verify Uploads

To list files in your bucket:

`$ aws s3 ls s3://my-linux-backup-bucket/`

To check contents recursively:

`$ aws s3 ls s3://my-linux-backup-bucket/ --recursive`

To check if a particular file exists:

`$ aws s3 ls s3://my-linux-backup-bucket/backups/data-backup-2025-08-16.tar.gz`

Useful AWS CLI Options for S3

Option	Description
--exclude	Exclude files matching a pattern.
--include	Include files matching a pattern.
--dryrun	Simulate the operation without performing it.
--delete	Delete files in destination not in source.
--storage-class	Set storage class (e.g., STANDARD, STANDARD_IA, GLACIER).

Security Best Practices

- Use IAM users with limited permissions for backup scripts.
- Enable MFA Delete for extra protection on buckets.
- Enable bucket versioning to prevent accidental deletion.
- Enable server-side encryption (SSE) when storing sensitive data: $ aws s3 cp file.txt s3://my-linux-backup-bucket/ --sse AES256.

Troubleshooting

Error	Solution
AccessDenied	Check IAM user permissions.
BucketAlreadyExists	Bucket names must be globally unique.
Command not found	Reinstall or update the AWS CLI.
Uploads fail	Check internet connection and file size limits.
cron not running	Check cron logs (/var/log/syslog or /var/log/cron.log).

Google Cloud Storage

Google Cloud Storage (GCS) is an object storage service by Google Cloud Platform (GCP) that offers high availability, durability, and seamless integration with other Google services. It's ideal for storing backups, logs, media, and large datasets.

Key Features

- 99.999999999% durability (11 nines, just like AWS S3)
- Different storage classes for cost optimization
- Lifecycle management to automate file aging and deletion
- Strong security and access control

Install the Google Cloud SDK (Includes gsutil)

Prerequisites:

- A Linux machine with internet access
- A Google Cloud account
- A billing-enabled GCP project
- Basic terminal experience

The gsutil command-line tool is part of the Google Cloud SDK.
Install with curl (recommended):

```
$ curl https://sdk.cloud.google.com | bash
```

Note This script installs the SDK in your home directory ($HOME/google-cloud-sdk). You'll be asked if you want to add the SDK tools to your shell profile (.bashrc, .zshrc, etc.)

Restart the Shell

Run

```
$ exec -l $SHELL
```

Alternatively, you can simply close and reopen your terminal.

Initialize the Google Cloud SDK

To start using the gcloud CLI with your Google Cloud account:

```
$ gcloud init
```

This command

- Opens a browser window for you to log in with your Google account
- Prompts you to select or create a Google Cloud project
- Configures default settings like region, zone, and output format

Running on Headless Servers (No GUI)

If you're working on a headless server (e.g., a remote VM or minimal OS), gcloud init may fail to launch a browser. Use the following alternatives.

Option 1: Manual Login via URL

```
$ gcloud auth login --no-launch-browser
```

This command outputs a link and a code:

1. Copy and paste the URL into a browser **on a different device**.
2. Log in with your Google account.
3. Paste the verification code back into the terminal.

Option 2: Use a Service Account (Recommended for Automation)

For scripts or automated systems, authenticate using a **service account**:

1. **Create a service account** in the GCP console.
2. **Generate and download a JSON key file.**
3. Authenticate using

   ```
   $ gcloud auth activate-service-account --key-file=/path/to/service-account-key.json
   ```

You can then set the project:

```
$ gcloud config set project YOUR_PROJECT_ID
```

Tip

- Use a dedicated GCP project just for backups to keep things organized.
- Use gcloud config list to review your active settings and credentials after setup:

  ```
  $ gcloud config list
  ```

Authenticate and Set Up Access

Log in (if you skipped gcloud init):

```
$ gcloud auth login
```

Set Your Default Project

```
$ gcloud config set project [PROJECT_ID]
```

You can find your project ID in the GCP console: https://console.cloud.google.com/.

Enable Billing (First-Time Setup)

Backups won't work unless billing is enabled. Go to
https://console.cloud.google.com/billing

Create a Google Cloud Storage Bucket

Create a Bucket

```
$ gsutil mb gs://my-linux-backup-bucket/
```

Bucket names must be globally unique (across all users).
You can specify a region:

```
$ gsutil mb -l us-central1 gs://my-linux-backup-bucket/
```

Choose Storage Class (Optional)

Storage classes affect cost and access speed:

- STANDARD: Default; good for frequent access.
- NEARLINE: Cheaper; access once a month.
- COLDLINE: Long-term storage; access once a quarter.
- ARCHIVE: Cheapest; retrieval takes hours.

```
$ gsutil mb -c nearline -l us-central1 gs://my-linux-backup-bucket/
```

CHAPTER 10 BACKUP AND DISASTER RECOVERY

> **Tip** Use NEARLINE or COLDLINE for backups that you rarely access.

Prepare Your Data for Backup

Check Data Size

```
$ du -sh /home/user/data
```

Optional: Compress Before Uploading

```
$ tar -czvf data-backup-$(date +%F).tar.gz /home/user/data/
```

This compresses the data into a file like data-backup-2025-08-16.tar.gz.

Upload to Google Cloud Storage Using gsutil

Google Cloud Storage (GCS) is an object storage service similar to Amazon S3. You can interact with it using the gsutil command-line tool, which is part of the Google Cloud SDK.

Upload a Single File

```
$ gsutil cp data-backup-2025-08-16.tar.gz gs://my-linux-backup-bucket/backups/
```

This uploads a single .tar.gz file into the backups/ folder in your bucket.

Sync a Directory

```
$ gsutil rsync -r /home/user/data/ gs://my-linux-backup-bucket/data/
```

Explanation:

- -r: Recursively sync subdirectories.
- Only **new or changed files** will be uploaded (based on size and checksum).

Important Note About Folder Placeholders

Google Cloud Storage is a **flat object store**, not a traditional filesystem. "Folders" are created virtually based on object names (i.e., data/file.txt appears under a data/ folder).

If a local folder is empty, gsutil rsync **does not create a placeholder folder** in GCS.

Example:

Let's say your local directory structure is

```
/home/user/data/
├── logs/            # empty
├── images/
│   └── photo.jpg
```

Run

```
$ gsutil rsync -r /home/user/data/ gs://my-linux-backup-bucket/data/
```

This will upload images/photo.jpg, but the logs/ folder **will not appear** in GCS because it has no files.

If an application relies on the presence of certain empty directories in GCS (e.g., for folder scanning or structure validation), you'll need to **manually create folder placeholders**, such as uploading a .keep file:

```
$ touch /home/user/data/logs/.keep
$ gsutil cp /home/user/data/logs/.keep gs://my-linux-backup-bucket/data/logs/
```

> **Note** Unlike aws s3 sync, gsutil rsync does not upload empty directories.

Sync and Delete Removed Files (Use Carefully)

```
$ gsutil -m rsync -d -r /home/user/data/ gs://my-linux-backup-bucket/data/
```

Explanation:

- -d: Deletes remote files that don't exist locally
- -m: Enables parallel/multithreaded operation for faster sync

> **Warning** Use -d only if you're sure you want to mirror the local state and delete from the cloud.

Automate with cron

Edit the crontab:

```
$ crontab -e
```

Add a cron job:

```
0 1 * * * /usr/bin/gsutil -m rsync -r /home/user/data/ gs://my-linux-backup-bucket/data/ >> /var/log/gcs_backup.log 2>&1
```

This runs daily at 1 AM. Logs output and errors to /var/log/gcs_backup.log.

> **Tip** Ensure the PATH to gsutil is correct. It might be in $HOME/google-cloud-sdk/bin/gsutil.

Restore Files from GCS

To download a file:

```
$ gsutil cp gs://my-linux-backup-bucket/backups/data-backup-2025-08-16.tar.gz .
```

To sync a full directory back to your machine:

```
$ gsutil rsync -r gs://my-linux-backup-bucket/data/ /home/user/data-restored/
```

> **Note** Always verify restored files by checking file sizes or hashes.

Security Best Practices

Use IAM Roles for Principle of Least Privilege

- Create a service account for automated backups.
- Assign it the Storage Object Admin role.
- Avoid using your personal account for cron jobs.

Enable Bucket Encryption

GCS encrypts data by default. For added security, you can

- Use Customer-Managed Encryption Keys (CMEK) via Cloud KMS.
- Or use client-side encryption (encrypt files before uploading).

Use Signed URLs (Optional)

To share a backup without public access:

```
$ gsutil signurl -d 1h private-key.json gs://my-linux-backup-bucket/backups/myfile.tar.gz
```

Verifying and Listing Files

List contents of a bucket:

```
$ gsutil ls gs://my-linux-backup-bucket/
```

List all files recursively:

```
$ gsutil ls -r gs://my-linux-backup-bucket/**
```

Check file metadata:

```
$ gsutil stat gs://my-linux-backup-bucket/backups/data-backup-2025-08-16.tar.gz
```

Access Control Options

You can manage permissions via

- Bucket-level ACLs
- IAM roles
- Uniform bucket-level access (recommended)

To give read access to a user:

```
$ gsutil acl ch -u user@example.com:R gs://my-linux-backup-bucket
```

Troubleshooting

Problem	Solution
403 Forbidden	Check IAM permissions.
gsutil: command not found	Ensure the SDK path is sourced.
Upload hangs	Add -m for multithreaded transfer.
cron not working	Check cron logs and paths to gsutil.
"Bucket already exists"	Use a globally unique name.

Backblaze B2

Backblaze B2 Cloud Storage is a reliable and cost-effective cloud storage service, well-suited for backups, long-term storage, and archival purposes. It's often favored for its simplicity and significantly lower pricing compared with Amazon S3 or Google Cloud Storage.

Why Choose Backblaze B2 for Backups?

- Low cost: Check current pricing here.
- S3-compatible API: Integrates easily with tools and workflows built for S3.

CHAPTER 10 BACKUP AND DISASTER RECOVERY

- Secure: Supports encryption, bucket-level access controls, and key-based authentication.
- CLI-friendly: Works seamlessly with rclone, a powerful open source tool for syncing files across cloud storage providers.

Install rclone on Linux

Prerequisites:

- A Linux system (Ubuntu, Debian, CentOS, Fedora, etc.)
- A Backblaze B2 account
- rclone installed and configured
- A basic understanding of terminal usage

rclone is a powerful and lightweight command-line program that supports over 50 cloud storage providers, including **Backblaze B2**, **Amazon S3**, **Google Drive**, and more.

Quick Install (Curl)

You *can* install rclone via the official install script:

```
$ curl https://rclone.org/install.sh | sudo bash
```

This script

- Downloads the latest stable release
- Installs rclone to /usr/bin/rclone

Note Piping install scripts directly into sudo bash is convenient, but potentially risky if the script changes unexpectedly. Instead, it's safer to **download, inspect**, and then run the script manually:

```
$ curl -O https://rclone.org/install.sh
$ less install.sh
$ sudo bash install.sh
```

Alternative: Verify Binary and Checksum Manually

For maximum safety:

1. Download the rclone release ZIP and checksum files from the official rclone GitHub releases page.

2. Verify the checksum using sha256sum.

3. Extract and move the binary to a secure location:

   ```
   $ unzip rclone-current-linux-amd64.zip
   $ cd rclone-*-linux-amd64
   $ sudo cp rclone /usr/bin/
   $ sudo chown root:root /usr/bin/rclone
   $ sudo chmod 755 /usr/bin/rclone
   ```

Other Option: Use Your Package Manager (May Be Outdated)

On some Linux distros, you can install rclone using your system's package manager.

Debian/Ubuntu

```
$ sudo apt update
$ sudo apt install rclone
```

RHEL/CentOS (via EPEL)

```
$ sudo dnf install epel-release
$ sudo dnf install rclone
```

These versions may lag behind the latest release—check rclone --version after install. Verify installation:

```
$ rclone version
rclone v1.65.2
- os/version: ubuntu 22.04
- os/kernel: 5.15.0
- os/type: linux
- go/version: go1.21
```

Note You can also install via your distro's package manager, but it may be outdated. Using the official script ensures the latest version.

Create a Backblaze B2 Account and App Key

Before configuring rclone, you need credentials from Backblaze.
Create an account.
Go to https://www.backblaze.com/b2/cloud-storage.html.
Generate app keys:

- Go to your B2 Cloud Console.
- Navigate to App Keys.
- Click "Add a New Application Key."
- Give it a name like rclone-backup.
- Set permissions (e.g., read/write access to a specific bucket or all buckets).

You'll get

- Key ID (like an access key)
- Application Key (secret)

Copy and save these; you'll need them for rclone config.

Configure rclone for Backblaze B2

```
$ rclone config
```

You'll be guided through a series of prompts.
Step-by-step configuration:

- Choose "n" for a new remote.
- Name the remote:
- Example: b2remote
- Select Storage ➤ type 6 or scroll to Backblaze B2.

- Account ID: Paste your Key ID.
- Application Key: Paste your secret key.
- Endpoint: Leave blank for default.
- Accept default advanced options (just press Enter).
- Choose Yes to test the connection.

You'll see the following:
Success! Remote "b2remote" is configured.

> **Note** rclone stores credentials in ~/.config/rclone/rclone.conf. Ensure only your user can access this file:
>
> ```
> $ chmod 600 ~/.config/rclone/rclone.conf
> ```

Create a Bucket (Optional)

If you didn't already create a bucket during app key creation:
Use the B2 Web Console:

- Go to Buckets.
- Click Create a Bucket.
- Name it (e.g., linux-backups).
- Choose private or public depending on use.

Or create via rclone:

```
$ rclone mkdir b2remote:linux-backups
```

This will create a folder (or bucket if it doesn't already exist).

Prepare Your Data for Backup

For instance, we want to back up the folder /home/user/data/:

```
$ tar -czvf data-backup-$(date +%F).tar.gz /home/user/data/
```

This creates a compressed file like data-backup-2025-08-16.tar.gz.

Back Up Data to Backblaze B2 Using rclone

Sync a Directory

`$ rclone sync /home/user/data/ b2remote:linux-backups`

This command will

- Create a mirror of the local directory in B2.
- Only upload new or changed files.

Copy a File

`$ rclone copy data-backup-2025-08-16.tar.gz b2remote:linux-backups/backups/`

Automate Backups with cron

To run regular automated backups:

Open the crontab:

`$ crontab -e`

Add a backup job:

`0 3 * * * /usr/bin/rclone sync /home/user/data/ b2remote:linux-backups --log-file=/var/log/b2_backup.log`

This runs daily at 3 AM and saves logs to /var/log/b2_backup.log.

Tip Make sure /usr/bin/rclone is the correct path by running which rclone.

Restore From Backblaze B2

Restore a File

`$ rclone copy b2remote:linux-backups/backups/data-backup-2025-08-16.tar.gz .`

Restore a Full Directory

```
$ rclone sync b2remote:linux-backups/ /home/user/data-restored/
```

> **Note** rclone will download only what's needed and skip already identical files.

Security Best Practices

1. Encrypt files before upload if storing sensitive data:

   ```
   $ gpg -c data-backup.tar.gz
   ```

2. Or use rclone crypt to transparently encrypt on the fly:

   ```
   $ rclone config
   ```

3. Keep rclone.conf permissions strict:

   ```
   $ chmod 600 ~/.config/rclone/rclone.conf
   ```

4. Rotate Backblaze app keys periodically.

5. Validate and monitor backups.

List Contents of a B2 Bucket

```
$ rclone ls b2remote:linux-backups
```

Check for Specific File

```
$ rclone lsf b2remote:linux-backups/backups/
```

Test File Integrity

```
$ rclone check /home/user/data/ b2remote:linux-backups/
```

This compares local and remote checksums.

Useful rclone Options

Option	Description
--dry-run	Simulate the action without executing.
--progress	Show transfer progress.
--log-file=FILE	Write logs to a file.
--bwlimit 1M	Limit bandwidth to 1 MB/s.
--transfers=4	Number of concurrent transfers.

Troubleshooting

Error	Fix
Failed to create bucket	Bucket name already exists or invalid.
invalid_auth_token	App key expired or incorrect.
File not found	Check spelling and path.
cron not running	Check cron logs (/var/log/syslog).

How to Test and Validate Your Backups

Don't just assume your backups work, test them regularly.

For tar Archives

```
$ tar -tvf backup.tar.gz   # List contents without extracting
```

For rsync

```
$ rsync -avnc /source/ /backup/   # Compare two directories
```

For rclone

```
$ rclone check /local/path remote:bucket/path # Compare remote and local directories
```

For S3

```
$ aws s3 ls s3://my-linux-backup-bucket/backups/ # List and compare expected backup files
```

Conclusion

In Linux system administration, data integrity and recoverability are non-negotiable. This chapter emphasized the critical role of backups and disaster recovery planning in maintaining system resilience. Whether you're safeguarding against hardware failure, user error, or a catastrophic event, a proactive backup strategy ensures your systems and data remain recoverable and your operations uninterrupted.

We've explored a variety of tools and techniques, from foundational utilities like rsync, tar, and dd to robust cloud-based solutions using AWS S3, Google Cloud Storage, and Backblaze B2 via rclone. Each tool has its strengths: rsync for efficient incremental backups, tar for archival storage, dd for full disk imaging, and cloud services for off-site redundancy and scalability.

Automation through cron ensures consistency, while practices like encryption, regular testing, and secure storage locations bolster the integrity of your backups.

Wrapping Up the Book

With this chapter, we've come to the end of our journey into the beginning of Linux system administration. From initial setup and user management to networking, security, automation, and now disaster recovery, each chapter builds upon the last to provide a practical, hands-on understanding of what it takes to run and maintain a secure, stable, and scalable Linux environment.

This book is designed to be a launching pad. Keep experimenting, stay curious, and remember: documentation is your friend, and community is your safety net.

If you've made it this far, thank you. I hope this book has helped demystify Linux system administration and inspired confidence in your own technical journey.

Index

A

Access control lists (ACLs), 34
ACLs, *see* Access control lists (ACLs)
Advanced Package Tool (APT), 77
    commands, 78
    Debian, 77
    DNF (Dandified YUM), 80
    Guix (GNU Guix system)
        functional packages, 88
        garbage-collection, 89
        installation/upgrading packages, 88
        roll-back, 89
    integration, 78
    Nix/Guix system
        command outputs/workflows, 86
        installation, 86
        legacy method, 86
        list installed packages, 87
        previous profile generation, 87
        recommended method, 87
        traditional tools, 86
    package information
        installation, 78
        lists, 78
        operation, 79
        search/remove options, 79
        upgrade option, 79
        version numbers and outputs, 80
    Pacman (Arch system)
        binary package, 84
        cache directory, 85
        dependency checks, 85
        installation, 84
        remove package, 85
        search option, 86
        sync/update, 84
    repos, 83
    third-party repositories, 83, 84
Amazon S3 (Simple Storage Service), 252, 253
Amazon Web Services (AWS)
    access/secret key, 255
    aws s3
        delete files, 257
        exact-timestamps, 258
        options, 259
        regular backups, 258
        restore files, 259
        security, 260
        troubleshooting, 260
        verification, 259
        versioning control, 258
    back up, 256
    bucket names, 256
    configuration, 255
    default region, 255
    download and installation, 253
    features, 253
    google cloud storage, 260, 261
    legacy regions, 256
    OS package management, 254
    prerequisites, 253
    S3 bucket, 255
    Security, 253

INDEX

Amazon Web Services (AWS) (*cont.*)
    single file, 257
    sync directory, 257
    timestamped file, 256
    upload data, 257
AppArmor, *see* Application Armor (AppArmor)
Application Armor (AppArmor)
    complain mode, 194
    edit profiles, 194
    enable/disable profiles, 193
    Logs, 194
    path-based access control, 193
    profile location, 194
    real-work scenario, 195
    rkhunter, 198
    rootkits, 196–198
    SELinux, 195
    status, 193
    working process, 193
APT, *see* Advanced Package Tool (APT)
Arch-based distributions, 2
Arch User Repository (AUR), 84, 98
Audit Daemon (auditd), 226, 227
AUR, *see* Arch User Repository (AUR)
AWS, *see* Amazon Web Services (AWS)

B

Backup/disaster recovery, 243
    AWS CLI v1 (*see* Amazon Web Services (AWS))
    business continuity, 243
    checklist, 244
    cloud storage solutions, 252
    compliance/legal requirements, 243
    data loss prevention, 243
    dd (disk duplicate)
        definition, 250
        device names, 251
        disk image, 250
        restore, 251
        restore image, 251
        supports status=progress, 252
        syntax, 250
        use cases, 250
        working process, 250
    rsync/rclone, 275
    rsync (remote sync)
        command, 247
        delta encoding, 244
        directory structure, 246
        incremental backups, 246
        link-dest path, 246
        location, 245
        remote server, 246
        syntax, 245
        use cases, 245
    strategies, 243
    tar
        compressed archive, 248
        extracting files, 249
        incremental backups, 249
        working process, 248
    tar archives, 275
    testing/validation, 275
Bootable USB drive, 5
    booting, 9
    Etcher, 5–9
    Linux
        confirm changes, 14
        distribution, 10
        erase disk, 13
        installation progress, 17, 18
        installation steps, 10
        interface, 11

keyboard layout, 11
location and time zone, 14
time zone, 15
Ubuntu Desktop, 11–13
updates/software, 12
user account, 16
post-installation, 18, 19

C

Chrony, 67
CLI, *see* Command-line interface (CLI)
Cockpit PackageKit plugin
   browser-based access, 99
   definition, 99
   features, 99, 101
   firewalls, 100
   installation/setup, 99
   NixUI/Guix web server, 100
   remote management, 100
   SELinux policies, 100
   web service, 99
Command-line interface (CLI)
   AWS (*see* Amazon Web Services (AWS))
   apt *vs.* apt-get, 68
   archiving and compression, 25
   built-in manuals, 22
   commands, 20
   disk usage and monitoring, 26
   file permissions, 23
   files and directories, 21
   Filesystem, 20
   graphical interfaces, 19
   networking, 24
   process management, 23
   SSH, 26
   terminals, 20
   viewing and editing files, 21

D

DAC, *see* Discretionary Access Control (DAC)
Debian-based distributions, 2, 77
DHCP, *see* Dynamic Host Configuration Protocol (DHCP)
Discretionary Access Control (DAC), 190–194
Distributions
   bootable USB, 5–19
   CLI (*see* Command-line interface (CLI))
   debian, 2
   definition, 1
   desktop/server, 3
   features, 1
   installation, 4
   ISO file, 4
   Red Hat–based systems, 2
   right information, 3
DNF (Dandified YUM)/RPM
   compatibility symlink, 80
   definition, 80
   package installation, 81
   remove/metadata, 81
   remove option, 82
   repositories, 80
   search, 82
   updates, 81
DNS, *see* Domain Name System (DNS)
Domain Name System (DNS), 65, 203
   command-line interface, 210
   dynamic IP addressing, 212
   /etc/hosts file, 210
   /etc/nsswitch.conf, 210
   hostnamectl, 211
   hostname/DNS (*see* Hostname/DNS configuration)

Domain Name System (DNS) (*cont.*)
    nameservers, 211
    Netplan, 213, 214
    static IP addressing, 212
Dynamic Host Configuration Protocol (DHCP), 10, 211

E

EPEL, *see* Extra Packages for Enterprise Linux (EPEL)
Etcher application, 6–10
Extra Packages for Enterprise Linux (EPEL), 143

F

FHS, *see* Filesystem Hierarchy Standard (FHS)
Filesystem Hierarchy Standard (FHS), 39
Filesystem management
    disk partitioning, 41
        fdisk, 42
    disk partitioning/dev/sdb, 42
    disk usage, 40, 41
    formatting partitions, 42, 43
    I/O disk, 46
    key directories, 39, 40
    monitoring disk health, 46
    mounting/unmounting, 43
        drive, 44
        /etc/fstab file, 44
        hibernation, 45
        swap space, 44, 45
    SMART disk health check, 47
Flatpak
    benefits, 90
    list/installation, 91
    uninstall packages, 91
Flatpak applications
    dual systems, 106
    Flatseal installation, 104
    GNOME Software, 106
    grant/restrict permissions, 105
    limitations, 104
    read-only access, 106
    sandboxed environments, 104

G

GCS, *see* Google Cloud Storage (GCS)
Google Cloud Storage (GCS), 260, 261
    account process, 261
    Backblaze B2
        account/app key, 271
        automated backups, 273
        backup.log, 273
        backups, 268
        binary/checksum manual, 270
        copying files, 273
        crontab, 273
        curl installation, 269
        rclone command, 273
        rclone configuration, 271
        rclone installation, 269
        restore file, 274
    bucket creation, 272
    bucket names, 263
    compressed file, 272
    cron job, 266
    data compress, 264
    data size, 264
    features, 260
    folder placeholders, 265
    gsutil tool, 261, 264
    headless server, 262

default project ID, 263
enable billing, 263
log in process, 263
service account, 262
URL *vs.* manual login, 262
local directory structure, 265
package management, 270
Debian/Ubuntu, 270
RHEL/CenOS, 270
restore files, 266
security
access control, 268
bucket encryption, 267
encrypt files, 274
IAM roles, 267
rclone option, 274
troubleshooting, 268, 275
URLs, 267
verification files, 267
shell, 261
single .tar.gz file, 264
storage classes, 263
sync/delete files, 265
sync subdirectories, 264
Graphical user interface (GUI), 3
Flatpak applications, 104–106
remote desktop, 227, 228
web-based tools, 95–99
GUI, *see* Graphical user interface (GUI)
Guix (GNU Guix system), 88, 89

H, I, J, K

Hostname/DNS configuration
communication, 203
distributions/custom setups, 206
editing process, 206
/etc/resolv.conf, 206
hostnamectl command, 204
local name mapping
/etc/hosts file, 205
/etc/resolv.conf, 206
modern distributions, 206
resolvconf, 207
symlink, 207
systemd-resolved
global section, 209
resolvconf, 210
services, 207
view process, 208
wlp2s0 interface, 209
terminal prompt, 204

L

Linux programming
AWS (*see* Amazon Web Services (AWS))
distributions (*see* Distributions)
filesystem structure, 39–48
package (*see* Package management)
system configuration, 49–73
user accounts, 29–37
Locales control, 69–71
Logical Volume Management (LVM), 10
Log management, 149
boot/hardware detection, 150
debugging service, 152, 153
rotation, 153
verbose, 153
high-resource processes
CPU/memory hogs, 154
iotop, 154
ports/services, 154
identification, 153
individual packages, 152
kernel, 150

INDEX

Log management (*cont.*)
   logrotate, 152
   messages, 150
   package management, 150
   rotation, 152
   syslog, 149
   systemd-based systems, 151
   /var/log directories, 149
   viewing process, 151
LVM, *see* Logical Volume
       Management (LVM)

M

MAC, *see* Mandatory Access
       Control (MAC)
Mandatory Access Control (MAC)
   AppArmor, 193, 194
   AppArmor/SELinux, 189–193
   SELinux, 190–192
Monitoring system performance
   browser, 162
   clarifications/troubleshooting
      command cheat sheet, 165, 166
      iostat/sysstat, 164
      iotop, 164
      memory metrics, 164
      netstat *vs.* ss, 164
   disk space, 146
   dstat, 143, 144
   essential tools and techniques, 137
   free (memory usage snapshot), 142
   htop, 138
   htop/top, 147
   iostat (input/output statistics), 140–142
   iotop, 148
   memory usage, 145, 146
   Netdata dashboard interface, 163
   performance optimization
      bleachbit, 155
      commands, 156
      critical directories, 156
      manual process, 156
      RHEL/CentOS, 157
      running services, 155
      stop/disable service, 155
      Swappiness controls, 157
      temporary files, 155
      tmpreaper, 156
   periodic historical statistics, 141
   pidstat/per-process, 140
   prerequisites, 149
   Resident Set Size (RSS), 148
   RHEL/CentOS/Fedora, 139
   system logs, 149–154
   top, 137
   top memory, 148
   troubleshooting, 140, 149
   tuning (*see* Tuning system parameters)
   vmstat reports, 139, 140
   web dashboard, 162
MySQL, *see* My Structured Query
       Language (MySQL)
My Structured Query Language
       (MySQL), 83, 84

N, O

Netdata dashboard, 162, 163
Netplan dashboard
   code information, 213
   configuration file, 214
   /etc/netplan, 213
   text editor, 213
   YAML files, 213
Networking/remote access

INDEX

data transfer, SCP and SFTP, 240–242
    troubleshooting, 240
Networking/remote access system
    Audit Daemon (auditd), 226, 227
    configuration, 203
    /etc/network/interfaces, 212
    graphical user interface, 227, 228
    hostname/DNS configuration, 203–212
    Netplan, 213, 214
    Red Hat systems
        CentOS Stream and Fedora, 214
        configuration, 215
        interface file, 215
        methods, 214
        nmcli, 214
        RHEL systems, 216
        static configuration, 216
    security, 233
    SSH, 218–226
    troubleshooting
        interfaces/IP addresses, 217
        logs, 218
        NetworkManager, 218
        restart interface, 217
        test connectivity, 217
    virtual network computing, 228, 229
    VPN, 233–237
    xRDP, 230–233

P, Q

Package management, 75
    AppStream, 77
    APT (*see* Advanced Package Tool (APT))
    comparative overview, 75
    concepts, 76
    edge cases, 103

    Flatpak apps, 104–106
    Snap/Flatpak/Native packages, 103
    graphical/web-based interfaces, 95–99
        Cockpit PackageKit plugin, 99–101
        Guix web interface, 102
        NixUI installation, 101
        Pamac, 98, 99
        security/auditing, 102
        synaptic package, 95–98
    PackageKit, 77
    Snap/Flatpak, 89–93
    tools, 75, 76

R

Red Hat Enterprise Linux (RHEL), 2
Remote access, *see* Networking/remote access)
RHEL, *see* Red Hat Enterprise Linux (RHEL)
Rootkit detection tools
    chkrootkit, 197, 198
    cron, 200
    monitor logs, 200
    rescue mode, 200
    rkhunter, 198
    scanning, 198
    source code, 199
    tools/code, 196–198

S

SCP, *see* Secure Copy (SCP)
Secure Copy (SCP), 241
Secure File Transfer, 242
Secure Shell (SSH), 218–226
    authentication, 221
    command-line interface, 26

INDEX

Secure Shell (SSH) (*cont.*)
    connection, 221
    Debian/Ubuntu, 218
    firewall status, 220
    installation, 218
    Linux Audit Daemon (auditd), 226, 227
    network connection, 52
    Red Hat/CentOS/Fedora, 219
    remote machine, 221
    remote/monitor access, 222
        events, 222
        failed logins, 225
        journalctl, 224
        log entries, 223
        login attempts, 225
        proactive monitoring tools, 226
        who/w/last, 223
    server configuration, 219
    service, 51
    service status, 219
    ssh-copy-id, 221
    testing, 222
Security, 167
    AppArmor/SELinux, 189–193
    auditd (monitor), 185
        audit.log, 188
        login/logout events, 186
        SSH configuration, 187
        step-by-step setup, 186
    authentication methods, 174
    availability, 167
    built-in/third-party tools, 169
    confidentiality, 167
    defense depth, 169
    definition, 168
    Fail2Ban
        check status, 185
        configuration file, 184
        definition, 183
        enable option, 184
        installation, 183
        IP information, 185
    firewall configuration, 170
        active rules, 173
        blocking ports, 173, 174
        default zone, 172
        distro, 170
        firewalld, 170, 172
        iptables, 170, 171
        nftables, 171
        packet filtering, 170
        setup, 170
    foundational pillars, 167
    integrity, 167
    IP address, 188
    least privileges, 168
    password authentication, 175
        cons, 175
        failed password, 177
        inactive accounts, 176
        pros, 175
        root login, 176
        secure process, 176
        strong passwords, 176
    principles, 168
    SSH key authentication
        asymmetric cryptography, 177
        definition, 177
        public key, 178
        server option, 179
        session, 174
        step-by-step process, 177
        testing process, 179
    status verbose, 189
    two-factor authentication, 180–183
    UFW access, 188

zero trust, 169
Security-Enhanced Linux (SELinux)
    commands, 191
    concepts, 191
    current mode, 190
    definition, 190
    GUI tools, 192
    logs, 192
    operational modes, 190
    type enforcement (TE), 191
    website files, 192
SELinux, *see* Security-Enhanced Linux (SELinux)
Server-side encryption (SSE), 260
SFTP, *see* SSH File Transfer Protocol (SFTP)
Shell scripting, 109
    automation, 119
        alerting system, 124
        csv file, 126
        full system backup, 119
        logging/compression, 120–122
        parse log files, 124–126
        reports, 125
        security updates, 121–123
        server resource, 123, 124
        user account, 126–128
    Bash, 112
    command interpreter, 112
    command substitution, 115
    conditional statements
        case statements, 116
        if, else and elif, 115
        tests, 116
    creation, 112
    cron
        backup process, 129
        commands, 128
        crontab file, 129
        editing process, 129
        entries, 132
        environment/permissions, 131
        journalctl, 132
        logging/output, 131
        scheduled backup, 133
        setup process, 134, 135
        solution, 131
        system-wide crontab, 132
        testing process, 133
        traditional syslog, 132
        troubleshooting, 133
        working process, 129
    debug mode, 119
    definition, 111
    echo/print, 115
    exit status, 118
    functions, 118
    interval system, 130
    logging errors, 119
    loops
        for loops, 116
        until, 117
        while, 117
    overview, 109–111
    returning values, 118
    running process, 113
    scheduling patterns, 130
    shebang (#!), 113
    system administrator, 111
    user input/output, 114
    variables, 113
        data type declaration, 113
        environment, 114
        quotes control, 114
Slackware-based systems
    building/installation, 93
    build system (xbps-src), 94

INDEX

Slackware-based systems (*cont.*)
    community-supported tools, 93
    CRUX (pkgmk, pkgadd, .tar.gz), 95
    definition, 91
    installation package, 92
    modern package managers, 92
    pkgtool, 92
    remove packages, 92
    sbopkg, 93
    slackpkg, 92
    slackpkg+, 93
    Solus (eopkg/eopkg, 94
    .tgz/.txz, 91
SLES, *see* SUSE Linux Enterprise Server (SLES)
Snap packages
    benefits, 89
    installation, 89
    list/remove packages, 90
SSE, *see* Server-side encryption (SSE)
SSH File Transfer Protocol (SFTP), 241
sudo, *see* Super User Do (sudo)
Super User Do (sudo), 29
SUSE Linux Enterprise Server (SLES), 3
Synaptic package management
    comprehensive view, 95
    desktop environments, 97
    features, 96
    Firefox, 97
    installation, 98
    package version, 96
System configuration
    automation, 71–73
        hardcoding passwords, 72
        non-interactive scripts, 72
        setup script, 71
        setup.sh, 71
    configuration, 49

locales control
    configuration screen, 70
    language, 70
    viewing process, 69
networking
    configuration tools, 61
    debugging issues, 64
    DNS resolution, 65
    interfaces, 62, 63
    IP address, 64
    safe test mode, 63
    setup, 61
    Ubuntu Netplan, 63
process management
    active processes, 56
    fields, 56
    htop output, 57
    interactive view, 57, 58
    job control, 61
    nice value, 60
    priority levels, 60
    ps aux command, 55
    running process, 58
    signals, 59
    system resources, 55
    tasks, 58
systemd, 49
    active, inactive, failed, 52–54
    connection, 52
    failed services, 54, 55
    services, 50
    SSH service, 51
    status, 50
    unit files, 50
    unit types, 50
time/time zone
    apt *vs.* apt-get, 68
    hardware clock, 68

ntp/chrony, 67
setup process, 66, 67
synchronization, 67
sync status, 68
system clock, 69

T

Tuning system parameters
drop-in config file, 160
file descriptors, 158
interactive terminal view, 161
long-term monitoring, 161
Netdata, 162
override file, 158
systemd-managed service, 158
TCP network, 159
backlog handling, 159
net.ipv4.tcp_tw_reuse, 159
network connections, 160
ulimit-n file, 159
user sessions, 158
2FA, *see* Two-factor authentication (2FA)
Two-factor authentication (2FA), 174
emergency scratch codes, 181
enable process, 180–183
factor, 180
login process, 183
PAM module, 181, 182
SSH server configuration, 182

U

User accounts
adduser command, 31
creation, 30
definition, 29
delete option, 32
file permissions, 34

group level, 33
chmod command, 34
chown, 35
groupadd command, 33
memberships, 33
home directory path, 32
password policies, 35
real-world scenario, 36
running process, 36, 37
SELinux context, 34
sudo, 29
useradd, 30
usermod, 31

V

Virtual machine (VM), 4
Virtual memory statistics, 139, 140
Virtual Network Computing (VNC)
contents, 229
desktop environment, 228
local machine, 229
remote machine, 228
SSH tunneling, 229
Ubuntu/Debian-based system, 228
Virtual Private Network (VPN), 233–237
account creation, 234
config files, 234
key pair generation, 239, 240
OpenVPN, 234
OpenVPN service
client, 235
connection, 236
credentials file, 236
service name format, 237
systemd, 236
remote networks, 233
test connectivity, 235

INDEX

Virtual Private Network (VPN) (*cont.*)
    WireGuard, 234
    WireGuard configuration, 237, 238

W

Web-based interfaces, 95–99

X, Y, Z

xRDP (Windows-compatible remote desktop)
    client side, 231
    installation, 230
    requirement, 231
    server side, 231
    session configuration, 230
    SSH tunneling, 231
    Windows/Remmina, 230
    X11 forwarding/Wayland
        common issues, 232
        session temporarily, 232
        Windows users, 233
        workarounds and solutions, 232

GPSR Compliance

The European Union's (EU) General Product Safety Regulation (GPSR) is a set of rules that requires consumer products to be safe and our obligations to ensure this.

If you have any concerns about our products, you can contact us on

ProductSafety@springernature.com

In case Publisher is established outside the EU, the EU authorized representative is:

Springer Nature Customer Service Center GmbH
Europaplatz 3
69115 Heidelberg, Germany

www.ingramcontent.com/pod-product-compliance
Lightning Source LLC
LaVergne TN
LVHW081537070526
838199LV00056B/3694